WHY ARE YOU SO-

Happy
Reading,

CATHY BURRELL

Cathy
Burrell

 FriesenPress

One Printers Way
Altona, MB R0G 0B0
Canada

www.friesenpress.com

ISBN
978-1-03-832177-0 (Hardcover)
978-1-03-832176-3 (Paperback)
978-1-03-832178-7 (eBook)

1. BIOGRAPHY & AUTOBIOGRAPHY, PERSONAL MEMOIRS

Distributed to the trade by The Ingram Book Company

For Baba.
The only person who I never wanted to be anything else.
I used to think 'home' was a place.
You taught me that 'home' was you.

PROLOGUE

"WHY ARE YOU SO *normal?*"

I was sitting across the table from a girl I'd gone to junior high and high school with. She had also modeled for me when I started my clothing store in 1990. She had moved to Vancouver, but we had kept in touch, seen each other at school reunions, and chatted briefly on Facebook. She was telling me all about her life and about a couple of big decisions she was grappling with now that she was divorced and not sure about the path forward.

She had had the kind of childhood I wished I'd had. A younger sister. Two parents who had divorced, but amicably, and had co-parented the two girls. Her mom had been a normal age when she had her, somewhere in her 20s, and they looked and acted like sisters. Shopping together, lunching together, hanging with the younger sister—you know, like a "normal" family.

Sitting and listening to her that day, I was surprised when she blurted out her question. I didn't have an answer. What's more, I knew that everyone in school had known about my strange family situation: A mom and dad who had lived in separate parts of Canada but stayed married. An alcoholic mother and estranged, much older brothers. Dad's three bankruptcies, and the purchase of an old run-down hotel in a small town up north that had turned him into a millionaire in his late 50s. A big extended family in Winnipeg, which included a whole bunch of other alcoholics, and a Baba who barely spoke English and thought I was the smartest, skinniest granddaughter on earth. My perceived privilege, driving new cars, and being gifted a house. High school boyfriend, now husband, no kids, successful business.

Sitting there at nearly 30 years old and thinking back on it all. I didn't think anything about my life up to that point could be considered normal at all.

PART 1: CALGARY

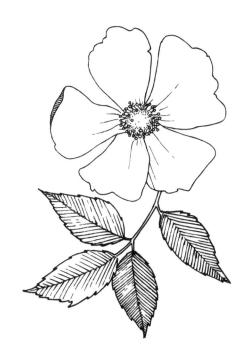

NORMAL

I WAS ABOUT two years old…

The stairs were hard and cold. I crawled up one at a time, and I could see my parents in the kitchen straight ahead. My mom was crying, and Dad was behind her, with his hand in the back of her hair, rhythmically banging her head into the brown wood kitchen cupboards. He was whispering to her, and I could see the sparkle of her wedding ring as she gripped the countertop.

Bang, bang, bang.

I heard David calling me and before I could turn my head, he had picked me up and thrown me over his shoulder. He kissed my cheek and asked if I wanted to watch some TV in the basement. He plopped me down in front of the black and white TV on the rug that covered the gray concrete floor, and threw himself onto the couch, furiously biting his nails.

Leaving Calgary the first time around 1973 was a wrenching experience, filled with all the drama of being ten, the youngest in a family of crazy people. I have told this story to nearly everyone I have ever met in my life, and as I get older I recognize how this one event changed the direction of my life. My father went bankrupt for the third time in Calgary. What started out as a fresh start in a new city turned into a nightmare. In the space of one week my dad went to jail for the weekend on tax evasion charges, our nearly brand-new Cadillac was impounded, and my mother's jewelry was seized by Revenue Canada.

My mother was suffering from depression, and the combination of antidepressants and alcohol had turned her into a zombie. She was there, but she barely spoke or ate. She just sat in a teal brocade swivel chair, in a living room that screamed early 1970s glamour—gorgeously over the top, with sheer curtains covered with teal-colored swagged drapes on the picture window—day after day, smoking and staring at the wall. That room was like a movie set. The chaos swirled around her, but never touched her, because only a little tiny bit of her was there.

Calgary is where I grew up. The city is where I became aware of who and why I was. When I had the chance to go back and live there again nearly 40 years later in 2014, I was excited and curious to see if my childhood had really happened and if my house and neighborhood really existed. I wanted to smell the lilacs, feel the north wind, see the mountains. I wanted to feel it all again, insulated from the confusion and pain and sadness. I wanted to feel the joy and the freedom that childhood and the big, blue Alberta sky had given me, standing like a giant on the top of Nose Hill with the soft, warm, brown cat's nose under my bare feet—at a comfortable, safe distance of 40 years ago.

As soon as our car arrived, we drove up 14th Street and turned right at the Calgary Winter Club, just past John Laurie Boulevard, where David used to take me driving and to the Dairy Queen on the corner. We turned onto Norquay Drive, and I saw the houses of my friends—and there it was. My old house. It looked smaller and nicer than I remember.

We drove down the hill to North Haven Elementary, and past the outdoor rink. We drove up the back alley and saw that the new owners had kept the giant lilac bush in the backyard, beside the garage, that had inspired my childhood bedroom décor: lilac-colored bedspread, drapes, and matching bed skirt.

I felt such a feeling of relief that the people living in that house had taken such good care of it. That house was the last place my family had lived together—and besides Baba's for a time, the only place I had felt safe and loved.

My childhood, that consisted of two seasons. The smell of lilacs in the spring, and when school was over, two tickets tucked into my report card that could only mean one thing—red cowboy boots and endless pleading for Dad or David to take me to the Stampede, as they were the most likely to win me a prize at a shooting game on the midway. I could still smell the corn dogs and mini donuts when Mom drove me to the airport for the long plane ride to Winnipeg to see Baba.

For eight summers, my life went on the same way. The house near Nose Hill. Friends from the elementary school at the foot of Norquay Drive. Phil's Pancake House near the bakery in Forest Lawn or in Banff every Sunday… and then, the summer I turned ten, Dad said we were moving.

I said no I wasn't, but when it was clear I had no choice, I asked where we were going. He said he'd gotten a job as the bakery manager in Yellowknife, a town in the Northwest Territories. I was even more confused, until he agreed to show me a driving map, and he unfolded it—*huge* on the basement floor—and pointed to a dot on a big lake, way up past Edmonton. I stared and stared at the map, and finally realized that at ten years old, I had no idea that there was any sort of land at the northern border of the provinces.

I asked him how we were going to get there, and he told me that we were going to drive, and it was going to take a couple of days, and part of the time we would be driving on gravel roads, and when we got to Hay River on Great Slave Lake, we were going to take a car ferry across to Yellowknife. He said that Puss-Puss was coming with us in the car but had to mostly stay in a cage, and that we would stop for the night somewhere north of Edmonton, he didn't know where. We were going to live in a big apartment above the bakery, and I had a nice room with a surprise in it.

Dad said that most of our furniture was going into storage, and I would be starting school in September in a new school in Yellowknife, so we had to leave pretty soon to get settled before school started—so I better start packing the things I wanted to take in the car because we were leaving on Monday because he had to start his new job.

For the next 35 years, every time I was on a plane that flew over Calgary, I would press my face into the plane window like a five-year-old and squeeze out a few tears.

Mom and Dad

MOM MET DAD while she was working as a nurse after WWII at the hospital in Plumas, Manitoba—a small village nestled in the Carberry Hills. Dad would be brought to the hospital either blind drunk or in the midst of some sort of seizure after a bit too much homebrew. They married in 1946.

So much happened before I was born in January 1963. Mom and Dad were married in one of those week-long farm weddings in Plumas, Manitoba, in 1946—right after the War in Europe ended. The boys were born shortly after the wedding, in 1948 and 1950. The three of us were born in different provinces, in different decades.

Mom's family had immigrated to Canada from Ukraine in the second wave of immigration in 1929. Dad was Ukrainian as well. In his family, I believe he was third or fourth youngest in a family of 13. The men in his family were bakers… and Dad was too.

I think Dad was a good baker and a bad businessman. By the time I was born he had gone bankrupt twice, and the worst was yet to come. Their married life had been constant fresh starts, constant conflict, constant battles for control.

Their relationship remained a mystery to me. As a kid, living in that house in Calgary, I could never decide if they loved each other or hated each other. I think that I was lonely in that house. My brothers got married when I was around six, and both moved out of the house around the same time. Dad was either working or sleeping, and Mom never slept, didn't eat much, and I usually found her in the same chair in the living room—sitting and smoking.

When I turned 40, my mom's second youngest sister—my least favorite—gave me the birth notification that Mom had mailed to her four decades before. *We did it. She is so cute.* God… she sounded so happy that she had birthed a little girl at nearly 40 years old.

There had been a million times over the years that I had questioned whether I was a wanted child. After all, they already had a family. Why would she have wanted the complication of a third child at her age? Her sons would never attend the same school, or have anything in common with this tiny baby… their baby sister. I questioned the strength—or lack of—in their marriage. I questioned the stability of the family, which right after I was born was moved briefly 1430+ miles away, finally settling afterwards for nearly 10 years 800+ miles away from my mom's family—in another brand-new city, in a new province.

I could never understand the logic—or the recklessness—of introducing me into a family situation that was never going to be anything but challenging, sometimes frightening, and always chaotic.

I always thought my mom was sad. A couple of years before she died, I blurted out that I was sorry that she was so unhappy. She replied that she wasn't unhappy. I took stock of the situation: Standing in that shabby little house in a small town, with her alcoholic son living in the house next door. Mom was nearly blind from macular degeneration, in constant pain from arthritis, asthmatic, and constantly bickering with Dad over the phone from Yellowknife. Waiting for him to fulfill his promise to—after 30 years of living apart—come home to live with her. But she wasn't unhappy? Perhaps it was me that was unhappy. Projecting how I would feel if I were her. I knew I would have been miserable.

That was how it started with us. Me not understanding why I had been born, and her not understanding why I worried about it.

The day before Mom died, when I was 36, Dad arrived to her home in Canoe, BC from his in Yellowknife. She had been unconscious for at least 48 hours when he opened the front door and yelled, "Lola, where are you?" as he put down his bag.

Somehow, she called back to him "Sam! I'm here," as he walked down the hall to her bedroom. When he walked back down the hall and flopped down in her chair, he looked at me and said that he was hungry. I got up and walked into the kitchen, never asking if she had said anything. David, Richard, and I just stared at each other, as we had been assembled at her house for days.

Maybe theirs was a love story...

CALGARY

I GREW UP in Calgary. From 1965 to 1975, it was my home. "Where are you from?" has never been an easy question to answer, as before Calgary there was Winnipeg and North Vancouver. After Calgary, there was Yellowknife, Abbotsford, White Rock, and Calgary for a second time—and soon, there will be Kelowna.

In Calgary for the first time, we lived in a new area in the northwest, right off 14th street. The house backed onto Nose Hill, and the neighbors on either side kept animals. Downstairs in one house, chinchillas. On the other side, in what seemed like a big backyard, a beautiful horse, bunnies, a dog, and at least one cat.

I was what was referred to in those days as a "menopause baby." When my mom told her sisters in Winnipeg that she was pregnant at nearly 41, they thought she was joking. They told me later that it was a good thing I looked exactly like my father; otherwise, the sisters would have started a rumor that the milkman was to blame. My brothers, David and Richard, were 13 and 15 years older than me, and Mom said that she used to make them change my diaper before they went out to play hockey or meet their friends.

Dad was a baker. He was from Ashville, Manitoba. When I was a kid, I told everyone that my dad was from Nashville… and after watching Sunday morning evangelicals on the black and white TV in the basement, I told everyone who would listen that Jesus was from Calgary, not Calvary. In 1965, Calgary represented an opportunity for a fresh start.

Childhood, for me, was North Haven Elementary. A couple of miles away, my brothers briefly attended James Fowler High. We were members of the Calgary Winter Club—also briefly, although I did learn to swim in that pool. My brothers took turns tossing me back and forth and after a few times sinking to the bottom, I learned to raise my arms and look to the light, breaking through the surface just as four pairs of hands were reaching down to grab me. I'm sure my mother's instructions to bring me back alive were in the back of their minds.

I learned to ride a bike on the hill that snaked down to the elementary school and have pictures of some sort of Community Day, proudly straddling my red bike complete with sparkly red banana-seat and sissy bar that David had helped me decorate with streamers in purple and yellow. I still have a cobalt blue bottle with silver decoration, much-faded now, that Richard bought for my mom one Mother's Day at the small convenience store across from the outdoor rink. I remember walking down that hill to school in morning snowstorms, and after school, dragging my fake fur-trimmed parka behind me up the hill while a chinook breeze worked to melt the snow.

I made lots of friends on my street, and knew all the neighbors. A group of girls and I tied our skipping ropes to the street lamp poles so we could take turns skipping double Dutch. We could skip until the streetlights came on.

Our last elementary school report card in June always included two tickets to the Calgary Stampede. I had red cowboy boots, and I was always excited to go to Stampede—especially the midway. If Dad took me, we always ate corndogs and those little mini donuts covered in cinnamon sugar. I didn't really care about the rides, but I was determined that Dad or David would win me the biggest stuffed animal. My brother was a better shot, and it seemed like the biggest stuffie prizes required a steady hand and good aim.

The house we moved into was new, and Mom asked what color I wanted my bedroom. The color would matter because matching the drapes to the bedspread was important to her. I wanted everything the color of the pale purple lilacs that bloomed each spring on the giant lilac bush beside the walk that led out of the backyard to the garage. The smell was so beautiful! Each time we had to take the car out, I flung myself as far into the bush as I could, inhaling deep, deep, breaths of sweet-smelling pale purpleness.

I loved that bedroom. I had a three quarter bed, with matching dresser and mirror. The floors and the furniture were almost the same dark honey color. I had a fluffy rug beside the bed, where I used to play with my Barbies, and a teal green and aqua striped sparkly vinyl covered armless settee. The far wall was all closets, and the window facing the backyard was high and wide.

In the winter I could hear the north winds howl, and in the spring with the window open and the curtains pulled back I could smell the lilacs and hear the birds singing. As soon as I opened my eyes in the morning, I was surrounded by the color of lilacs and no matter the season could imagine the scent.

I slept in that room for nearly ten years—the only bedroom I ever remembered—and would have happily stayed there forever.

I received a brand-new Barbie one Christmas. She was blonde and tanned, and she was from somewhere called Malibu, in sunny California, according to the package. Next to my Easy-Bake oven, Barbie was my favorite. I can't remember her outfit, although I think it was some sort of striped top and a pair of pants that ended just below her knee. She arrived with her own carrying case, which I thought of as her swingin' apartment, complete with a place she could stand up in so I could close the case with her in it, grab the handle, and take her *anywhere*... even though truthfully she never left my bedroom. She also had a hanging bar for clothes, and two drawers, which I think I put her high-heeled pink slide shoes in.

Barbie and I had many conversations on the fluffy rug next to my bed over the next few years. I asked her about Ken, and her friend

or niece Skipper, and I wanted her to tell me all about Malibu…
especially on days when the north wind howled around the back of
the house and the snow piled up in drifts, nearly up to the bottom
of my bedroom window.

At some point in the future, I received another Barbie. She had
long dark hair and a boring outfit, and came in a case that was
twice the size—supposedly to make this Barbie and Malibu Barbie
roommates. Both Barbies could stand on either side of a much
bigger closet, with a double hanging bar, which could accommodate
tops or minidresses on the top bar and shorts or miniskirts on the
bottom bar. There were also *four* big drawers. I didn't care for the
new Barbie, nor her gargantuan two-bedroom case. Malibu Barbie
and the smaller case were perfect as they were.

When my husband changed jobs in 2014, at 50—the same age
my dad had been when we left Calgary in the middle 70s—we
purchased a small, 600-square-foot apartment on 12th Street in the
Beltline. The apartment faced north, and I could see 14th Street and
Nose Hill from our living room.

We knew that Calgary wasn't going to be where we retired, as I
had no family left in the city, and when he accepted the job, he had
never been to Calgary. I had gone back to school to get a teaching
certificate in BC and didn't join him right away. He proceeded to
make the little apartment home, buying furniture and getting the
kitchen organized. When he opened the door the first time, all I
could think was that this apartment was the cutest little Barbie case
I never knew I'd wanted, and had missed.

My family had arrived in Calgary via Winnipeg, with a brief stop
in North Vancouver after Dad had gone bankrupt for the second
time. He got a job after that bankruptcy on the top of Grouse
Mountain working as a cook. I don't remember that house, but
years later David drove me there when we were living in Abbotsford
and showed me the house and the creek that ran through the front
yard. He told me that we had had a big black cat named Blackie,
who had died shortly after we moved to Calgary. I don't remember

Blackie, except for a grainy old black and white photograph of me holding a cat that lengthwise was almost as tall as I was, in one of those "kid grabbing the poor cat and almost strangling him" poses. But when I met Barbara Hilland in Calgary, and started going over to her house to play, she had a big fluffy cat—and I started asking Mom if we could get one.

We had a cleaning lady who had a cat that had just birthed a litter of kittens, and we went over to see them one morning. I picked a white one with big brown and black patches, with a mostly white face, with a beautiful walnut-brown nose. She was extremely fluffy, with big green eyes, and I named her Puss-Puss. She grew into the most beautiful cat, with magnificent whiskers and a sweet disposition. She lived in Calgary and Yellowknife and Abbotsford and died when she was the ripe old age of 16.

My birthdate was problematic when it came to starting school. At that time Calgary did not offer kindergarten, and I was a smart, chatty little five-year-old who loved to learn. Mom found a private kindergarten called Christopher Robin, and I was enrolled the September I turned five. I needed to wear a uniform, and as soon as it was ready, pictures were taken. Me posing with my chin on my chubby fist, seated on the settee in my bedroom, my hair freshly cut, smiling my biggest smile, missing two front teeth. Mom would drop me off in the morning, and Dad would usually pick me up in the afternoon.

One day, after Mom had pulled away, I tried the front door to the school and it wouldn't open. I tried again. No luck. For some reason, I decided that I would walk to the bakery. I thought I knew what street it was on, what direction to go, so I did. I remember the day was warm, and it did feel like I had walked a long way, but at some point that morning I did arrive at the bakery.

When I pulled open the glass door and the little bells that were attached to the door jingled, the first person I saw was Aunty Jan—she worked at the cash register. She took one look at me and yelled into the back, "Sam! She's here!" and Dad came walking out of the back room. My legs were tired, and I was a little thirsty. When Dad came over to me, he asked me where I had been, and even swung the door open again—*jingle, jingle*—looking for a car in the parking lot that might have dropped me off. He told me that Mom had been worried, and asked me why I didn't go to school, and I guess at this point I thought I was in trouble. He was speaking so quietly, not directly to me, so I started to cry.

He lifted me up onto a stool in the back where the other guys were working, got one of them to bring me a cupcake from the freezer, and got me a glass of water. He walked over to the phone on the wall and made a call. Aunty Jan—she wasn't really my aunt, just a woman who had worked for Dad, a tiny, round woman with dark curly hair and a Scottish accent—came over to bring me a Kleenex and tell me that everybody was worried about me because my teacher had called and asked why I wasn't in school. And Mom had called Dad, and then drove back to the school and all around the neighborhood looking for me.

I kept crying because my legs felt really heavy, and I was scared that Mom would be mad, and Dad and Aunty Jan kept talking about how I couldn't have walked five miles to the bakery all by myself while they looked at my dusty shoes and my tear-stained face. Dad said that it was OK, and that he would drive me home. When he helped me off the stool, I could hardly stand up, and he put his big hand on my back and said, "Come on." Mom was at home waiting for me.

DINNER

MY BEST FRIEND was Barbara Hilland. She lived down the street on the opposite side in a house that was bigger and nicer than our house. They had lived there longer than we had, and she had a couple of older brothers too, one who was the same age as David. Mr. Hilland, Barbara's dad, was tall and thin, and the entire family was blonde. Barbara's hair was so blonde it was almost white, and it was long and shiny, and her mom and her used to fight about braiding her hair every morning. Barbara told me one day that her mom was really her step-mom, as her mom had died after a long illness. Her step-mom was the housekeeper who had helped look after Barbara's mom at home when she was sick.

I don't think it had been long since her mom had died, and as the only girl, I think she really missed her. Every time she spoke about her mom, she always looked up—because I guess she thought her mom was watching her from heaven—or she would get tears in her eyes and try not to cry.

Barbara was a couple of years older than I was, and we liked to play at her house. She had a playroom with lots of toys and books and puzzles, and because the playroom was on the main floor, the room was warm—unlike my basement at home. She had a big old fat cat, who was always sleeping, but always woke up and meowed at the door so Barbara would let her in and she could find a spot to sleep where we were playing.

I have always liked to have one friend at a time, and Barbara was my first friend on that street. I was always at her place. Once in a while I would stay there so long that Hazel, Barbara's step-mom, would ask if I wanted to stay for dinner, and I always said yes. She would call my mom to make sure it was OK, and we would help set the table.

The kitchen was at the back of the house beside a nice dining room with a bay window looking out into their big backyard. Hazel would make different food than we had at home, and I was fascinated by the little plate of cut up vegetables and olives that she would put on the table, that everyone was allowed to eat before we ate dinner. Mr. Hilland owned a gas station down the hill past our school, and he came home for dinner every night—*at the same time*! The boys also were at home because they were going to high school and were usually in their rooms studying before dinner. When Mr. Hilland got home, he always said hello to me, and kissed Hazel on the cheek, and Barbara too, and after he had cleaned his hands he would call the boys down for supper. He would still be wearing his uniform from work, with the patch on his left side that said Alan and on the right side Esso. The boys would come downstairs and say hi to me and to their dad, and we would say grace, and Mr. Hilland would start passing the food.

They would all chat with each other, and smile and laugh, and eat, thanking Hazel for another great meal. I used to sit there in the glow of the dining room lamp, looking at all of them together, being nice to each other, in that pretty room that had wallpaper and a sideboard with a wedding picture of Hazel and Alan right beside a picture of Barbara's mother, and feel so happy and content and calm… and wonder why my family wasn't like them.

I can barely remember what our kitchen looked like in the house on Norquay Drive, but I remember a small Arborite table where I received my one and only spanking from my dad because I went to Barbara's place one day but forgot to tell anyone.

It was getting dark, and I could hear Hazel in the kitchen starting to make dinner. It was like slow motion. I suddenly realized that Mom hadn't been home when I left the house a few hours ago, and that David had been snoring in his room downstairs. I stood up and turned my head to look out of Barbara's playroom window just as the street lights came on. And I saw *my* father, in his white shirt tucked into his gray pants with his black belt and matching brogues—the ones with the little holes that made a pattern—walking up and down the street. Seeing him walking on the street was like seeing a bear in a shopping mall. It just didn't make sense. Dad did many things, but walking wasn't one of them.

I don't even remember saying goodbye to Barbara. I was in such a panic. I grabbed my coat and ran outside, and when Dad saw me, he stopped to glare at me, with a slight smirk on his face. I ran over to him talking, shouting that I was really sorry, and Mom wasn't home, and David was sleeping. I should have left a note, but I didn't think that I would be out so long, and I guess I could have called, but we were playing Barbies... He looked down at me, grabbed the hood of my winter coat and pulled me down the street without looking at me. Dad told me that I was in big trouble and that Mom didn't know where I was and had called him at the bakery to come home and find me, and that I was gonna "get it" when we got home.

That walk up to our front door seemed to take an hour, and I was already sobbing. Dad opened the front door and let the blue screen door slam behind us, while yelling to Mom that he'd found me and that we were going up to the kitchen for a spanking. I had been threatened with a spanking many, many times, but the worst that had ever happened was that Mom had grabbed one of my arms and had given me a shake. I don't know why, but when she shook me, I would always go limp and fall to the floor, like she had killed me. That used to make her even madder, and she would tell me to get up, and if I didn't, she would stalk off muttering in Ukrainian under her breath.

Dad sat down heavily in one of the much-too-small kitchen chairs and motioned that I was supposed to lay over his legs on my stomach. I considered asking for more information, but he had that look on his face, so I flopped down over his legs, my head nearly touching the floor. Then he leaned down and whispered that when he slammed the table with his hand, I was supposed to yell really loud. For the next few minutes, the slamming and yelling continued while I tried not to laugh between wails of anguish, until Mom came upstairs to see what was going on. By this time, I had gotten a nosebleed, but despite the smile on his face and the blood and snot all over my confused face, it was clear our performance had been unconvincing. She gave both of us a couple of whacks, while he roared with laughter and protested, saying that he had done what she wanted, found me, and given me a good spanking... calling her *Lubichka* and asking her what was for dinner.

We never ate at the same time or together as a family. Mom or David made me breakfast each morning. I always walked home from school at lunchtime for a sandwich or some soup, and to visit with Mom, who asked me questions about what was happening in my school day. I'm not sure how many kids stayed in school at lunch or ate quickly and went outside to play with other kids, but I seemed to be the only kid walking up the hill at lunch time. Dad was always gone when I got up in the morning, and David was usually sleeping. By the time I noticed, Richard had probably already moved out. After school, Mom was at home as well, and she and I ate dinner early, as we didn't know what time Dad was coming home. After supper, David was usually getting up and sometimes going out, so he never had dinner with us. And when I say us... it was usually me, on my own, downstairs in front of the black and white TV, with a TV tray and a TV dinner! The fried chicken ones were my favorite, but I wasn't exactly a fussy eater.

Mom never really ate. I think she was always watching her weight or wasn't hungry or didn't think eating was important. She had a lot of health problems starting with a hysterectomy, and she smoked a lot and probably couldn't taste anything and maybe felt that she had no one to cook for. Dad always needed dinner whenever he got home, but again, I remember eating with him in restaurants but never at home. Maybe I was in bed? I know he liked tea after dinner, and something sweet after his meal. He used to love canned fruit with whipping cream. Despite the fact that he owned a bakery, he very seldom brought anything home for us. He was a big man, and I was a chubby little kid, and Mom was trying to stay slim, so when I asked about pie or cookies or cupcakes from the bakery, she always used to say "Cathy, you don't need that."

Mom became a diabetic in Calgary. We went to the garden center down the hill from the airport one Sunday morning, and we were wandering around in one of those big greenhouses with sawdust on the floor, and I was running all over the place pointing out plants I thought were pretty, and she said, "Cathy... I'm seeing spots before my eyes... I think I'm going to faint..." and before I could turn around to ask what the spots looked like, she was lying on the ground.

I ran over to her, but she wasn't moving, even after I gave her a shake, so I ran towards the woman in front of me to tell her that my mom had fainted. She went running over to where Mom was laying on the ground, and I ran after her. She asked me what my mom's name was, and I told her, and she started saying "Lola, Lola, can you hear me?" She said that she was a nurse and told me to run over to the cash registers and tell someone that they should call an ambulance.

I ran as fast as I could, and I was out of breath by the time I got to the cash desk and declared in my loudest voice that my mom had fainted and we needed an ambulance, and started to run back to where she had collapsed.

Two men ran past me asking where she was. I pointed, and by the time we got back to Mom and the nurse, Mom was sitting up, looking very pale. Mom had told the nurse that she had been diagnosed with diabetes but hadn't eaten since last night and didn't want to go to the hospital and asked if one of the men could drive us home. One did, and the man and my mom chatted in the front seat, and I sat in the back seat with my heart still pounding. I kept asking Mom if she was going to faint again, and she said not to worry, we would have some toast and some juice, and she would be fine.

When we got home, we woke David up and told him what happened, and he drove the man back to the nursery, and Mom plugged in the kettle to make some coffee and found some bread to make us some toast.

Mom and I

MOM AND I rarely argued—unlike Dad and David, or Dad and Richard, or Dad and Mom. I generally did as I was told, as I never really imagined an alternative, and I so hated the constant yelling and screaming, and stomping around that I thought agreeing was a great alternative. Mom had waited a long time to have a girl, and she had always been a very girly girl. She always dressed nicely, wore the proper undergarments, did her makeup before going out, and had beautiful special occasion clothes.

Under the stairs in the basement was a small cupboard, with a lightbulb hanging from the ceiling with a piece of string hanging from it that if I stood on tiptoes, I could reach to turn on the light. The entire closet was filled with dresses. Mom's old dresses that she used to wear to dances, or weddings, or out to beer parlors. They were every shade of pastel—pale blue, lilac, yellow, pink—and the skirts were satiny on the outside and full of scratchy netting on the inside that make the skirts stand out like an open umbrella. I used to open that closet door every once in a while to feel around the fabrics, and look at the tiny little sequins, and what looked like diamonds glued onto the top parts of the dresses.

She never wore those dresses that I can remember. Mom used to always wear a black dress on the rare occasion that she and Dad went out anywhere at night without me. She always wore bright red lipstick and perfume—Chanel No. 5—and she always carried a special sparkly little purse that contained her cigarettes, lighter, and lipstick. When she would come into my bedroom to tell me that they were leaving, she would give me a kiss, and I always loved the way she smelled. Like hairspray and Chanel No. 5 and Peter Jackson cigarettes. I still have two of those little purses, and even 40 years later, they still smell like her.

Tragically for my mother, her only daughter was not even a teensy bit girly. I was sloppy and messy and rumpled, and I wore the first thing I laid my hands on in the morning, in order to get out the door to school—where all the fun was.

I didn't understand her fixation with picture day. I would receive the flyer with the date and would promptly leave it on my desk or throw it in the trash can on the way up the hill on my way home for lunch. The day would come, and I would have my picture taken, and a week or so later receive the pictures, and take them home to show Mom. She would be horrified! Mortified! And the lecture would begin.

My first kindergarten pictures, taken when I was five while I was attending Christopher Robin, were her favorites. She'd hired a photographer who had come to our house and taken pictures of me in a variety of poses in my school uniform, with my freshly washed face and pixie-cut hair smoothed and shiny (with both front teeth conspicuously absent).

Those first pictures must have set some sort of expectation that I liked having my picture taken. I didn't mind having my picture taken; I objected to the time it took to shop for a new outfit, try on clothes at Simpson Sears, and have those clothes pinned and altered, and have my hair cut and styled the morning of the pictures while wearing said itchy, weird outfit! (My cousin Patty commented once, after receiving my grade 3 picture, that I looked like a 40-year-old divorcee.)

So from grades 1 to 4, I always had two sets of pictures. There was one that I had taken when Mom didn't know it was picture day—messy hair, plain white sweater with a breakfast ketchup stain on it, faded pants a size too big, and a half smile with my eyes facing left or right because one of my friends had walked in, and I wanted to know what number they were in line… And then there was the "perfect" set of pictures that my mother insisted on. New outfit, combed and curled hair, crazy outfit that I would *never* wear again—as really, was I going to wear it to skip double Dutch or chase gophers on Nose Hill? But Mom always sighed happily, when I brought home the "preferred pictures." She always tried to convince me that I looked so nice when I made an effort… even though it was she who had made the effort!

In the 80s when I was around 18, she gave up trying to get me to wear what she wanted, look nice, wear nylons, put on makeup or even a bra. I had an event I had to go to, and she told me that she didn't have the strength. She threw me her credit card, and told me to buy whatever I wanted—she didn't care.

I don't know what possessed me. Maybe my new boyfriend, maybe being alone to choose, but I went to the mall—to Eatons, to the Brass Plum section—and purchased a cream silk blouse, a green, cream, and black plaid bias-cut wool skirt, a deep green cotton velvet blazer, and black knee-high boots with a bit of a heel. I wore Baba's rose gold earrings, and modeled the outfit for her when I got home. She had me turn around a couple of times and told me that she loved the outfit and I looked fantastic in it. Then she climbed off her bed and told me that she wanted to take my picture, downstairs in the living room, and said I should get the camera.

More than 20 years after she died, I was cleaning out her closet and in the far back corner, in a yellowed dry-cleaning bag, was the blouse, the skirt and the blazer, along with a few other long dresses I had worn to my graduation and a couple of dances. I lost track of her dancing dresses after we moved to Yellowknife, but she had hung onto my much more modern, modest outfits. I'm guessing to remind her that once in a while her only daughter took the time to dress up and look nice.

Mom and I used to go out to do the grocery shopping every week after she went to the beauty salon to have her hair done. It was our Friday routine that stayed the same for years—until one day after groceries, we stopped at the liquor store in North Hill Mall. I had my door halfway opened before she told me that I would have to wait in the car, as kids weren't allowed in the liquor store, but she would be right back. She came out a few minutes later with a bottle of red wine in a brown paper wrapper and a case of 12 beers in a cardboard container with a handle. She put everything on the floor in the back seat, and I listened to the bottles *jingle* all the way home.

I don't know if I asked why we stopped there, but a new routine was formed.

I never recall seeing my mom drinking in Calgary, but sometimes she had a strange look on her face, kind of glassy-eyed not looking at me when she spoke. I also remember her cheeks being red—and I noticed that because my mother had beautiful pale skin.

One night after supper, before Dad got home, Mom said that we had to go out. It was like she was telling me we were going to the moon. We *never* went out after dark! Once in a very long while, Mom would put on a knee-length black dress with a two-strand string of pearls. She used to wear red lipstick and spritz herself with Chanel No. 5 perfume. She would walk into my bedroom looking beautiful, in her high black heels, and tell me that Richard Symington's sister was downstairs and would look after me while she and Dad went out.

She wasn't dressed up this night—in fact, she looked like she had been crying—and she put on a sweater, and told me to put on my shoes because we wouldn't be long. I think we drove downtown, not down 14th Street, but down Centre Street and over the bridge with the two concrete lions all lit up in the darkness.

We stopped at a building in an alley, and after we parked, she told me that she was going to a meeting for other people with drinking problems, and I should come inside with her, as it would only be a half an hour. I was so mad! Maybe I was tired or a little scared because Dad wasn't there. I didn't want to go and sit in a meeting with a bunch of people I didn't know, and I had no idea why she would want to meet with people who had a drinking problem, whatever that was.

She spoke quietly to me, and her eyes were pleading, but I crossed my arms over my chest and absolutely refused to get out of the car. I think she had seen that look on my face before and knew that I would not budge. She sighed and told me not to get out of the car. She was going to lock me in the car, and take the keys, and she would be back as soon as the meeting was over. By this point I was in a full pout and wasn't speaking to or looking at her.

I sat there in the quiet and looked around the alley. No one was around, and I climbed back and forth from the front seat to the back, lying down in the back seat, not even reaching the far door. The back seat of that car had trays that dropped down behind the front seats, where when we bought the car and Dad had taken us to Dairy Queen, I had spilled my strawberry sundae on the brand-new upholstery, and sat on the stain to cover it up.

I must have fallen asleep because when I woke up we were driving home, back over the Centre Street Bridge, this time facing the lovely concrete lions, their mouths open in a full roar. Not a word was spoken, but for the rest of my life, I regretted not going into that first meeting with her because as I got older I realized how difficult it must have been for her to take me with her that night, and how she was probably doing it for me.

For a few months after that first meeting (she never asked me to go with her again) we didn't stop at the liquor store on Fridays. I think that Dad thought that Mom not drinking was funny because a couple of times when we ate supper together, Dad would ask her to bring him a beer, and he would make a big deal about pouring the beer in the glass and taking a big drink and then letting out a very loud, theatrical, "Ahhhhhh!" And then a big laugh.

Mom used to look at him and then me, and in a low, quiet voice say something to him in Ukrainian, and he would laugh again.

Right up until we left Calgary, I would sometimes ask Mom to sleep with me in my lilac bedroom at the back of the house. She always said yes. One of those nights she told me that she was going to teach me a prayer, and we were going to say it together. I remember that she was holding my hand really tight, and then she began whispering, "God, grant me the serenity to accept things I cannot change…"

BICYCLES

WHEN WINTER TURNED to spring in Calgary, the bicycles came out. I saw other kids racing up and down the street, riding all the way up to 14th Street and up onto Nose Hill, following the trails to the top, or speeding down the middle of Norquay Drive down the hill towards the school, swerving onto the sidewalks dodging cars coming up the hill.

I wanted a bike, and one day David arrived with a roar and pulled a brand-new bike over his headrest on the passenger side of the car and out of the open window. It was the prettiest bike I had ever seen! It wasn't a little girl's pink bike with training wheels. This bike was bright red, with a red, glittery banana-seat with a sissy bar and tall handlebars with a sort of crook in the middle. The handlebar grips were the same glittery red as the seat, but in a soft sort of jelly material, and hanging from the grips were red glittery strips that fluttered in the breeze, There was a humped bar in the middle, and a red kickstand.

By the time he had the bike on the ground, I was hopping up and down, screaming for him to let me sit on it. He leaned it over so I could swing one leg over, and once my bum was on the seat, he tilted it upright. It was clear that it was a little too tall for me because when I sat on it, my feet didn't quite touch the ground. The seat wasn't adjustable, and I certainly wasn't going to have him take it back to the store to get a smaller one, so I asked him to push me along so I could get the hang of pedaling. He hung onto the sissy bar and pushed me up and down the flat part of the street a couple of times, but he was winded, as he had been smoking for a few years already. I also wasn't light, and he was trying to keep me and the bike upright, which wasn't an easy feat. He pushed me up onto the sidewalk parallel to our front lawn, and let go so I fell over onto the grass—when I howled in protest, he stood there with his hands on his hips, huffing and puffing, and telling me that he would get some kid in the neighborhood to teach me how to ride, but he had to go, and I was supposed to walk the bike up the front steps and into the house so it wouldn't get stolen.

Before I could untangle myself, he was back in the car, and with a rumble and a squeal of tires he was gone. I managed to push the bike up the grassy hill that was my front yard, but I couldn't maneuver it up the steps or into the house, so I opened the screen door and yelled for Mom to come and help me. She said that when Dad got home he would help me learn to ride, and we each took a handlebar and pushed the bike around the side of the house and into the backyard. I activated the kickstand, and stood back to admire this beauty of a bike.

When Dad got home, he had a look at the bike and said we should take it out to the street just as the streetlights were coming on… and to my embarrassment, he swung his leg over and had a seat, and I screamed, as I could see the tires flattening with his weight. He got off, laughing at the look on my face, and told me to get on.

He pushed me like David had earlier, and as David had earlier, ran out of breath, and for 15 seconds I pedaled on my own, and then fell, scratching some of the red paint and scraping the side of my knee. He also said that tomorrow after school he would have some kid from the neighborhood teach me to ride.

I still have scars on my knee from learning to ride that bike, but some kid did teach me, and I grew into it, and spent many a summer night riding around the neighborhood, on my own or with any kid who rode past me on his way to wherever.

That bike was everything. It was freedom to explore and freedom to get as far away from the house as I dared—and sometimes a little further. Like everyone else in my family, I now had a vehicle. A means of escape. Two wheels and the stillness of a warm summer night.

Medical Mishaps

WHEN I WAS around seven, my Aunty Ann from Vancouver mailed me a parcel for my birthday. Mom was in the kitchen making dinner, so I grabbed a big kitchen knife and took the parcel over to the dining room table and proceeded to saw away at it. The package was rectangular, maybe a foot long, and the entire thing was wrapped in tape. I grabbed one end and proceeded to try to cut it open, like you would cut a slice of bread from a loaf.

The knife slipped on the tape and sliced into the fat part of my left index finger. There was a sharp pain, and I pulled out the knife, and stuck my finger into my mouth. Mom heard the knife drop and turned around to see me standing there, with my left index finger in my mouth and blood starting to drip down my chin, and screamed. She walked me over to the kitchen sink and told me to spit out the blood while she had a look at the cut. She wrapped a tea towel around the now-throbbing finger while she went to the bathroom to find some gauze. The finger was wrapped, and when Dad got home from work Mom wanted to take me to the hospital for stitches.

Dad had a look and said it didn't look too bad, and that I didn't need stitches—something that I had been telling Mom for the last hour. At school the next day, it was hard to miss the huge white bandaged finger, and I cheerfully took off the outer gauze layer to show anyone who wanted to see how I had very nearly cut the finger right off, but my mother had stuck it back on, and when they saw the inner layer of gauze soaked with blood... they all agreed it was the grossest thing they had ever seen.

I was always sick as a kid in Calgary. Everyone in the family smoked—in the house, in the car, day and night. I had sore ears and a sore throat for a few months, when I was around four, and a persistent cough. It was decided that I should have my tonsils removed. Mom had been a nurse until she got married, and didn't like the idea of her little girl having an operation, but knew she wouldn't be able to be at the hospital all the time. She arranged to hire a night nurse for the two days I would be in the hospital so someone would be there in case I woke up in the night scared and alone.

A couple of times I woke up with a sore throat after Mom had left for the night, and the nurse would say she would be right back and come back with a popsicle! In the operating room, the doctor had a very deep voice, and I wasn't really scared to have the operation because I asked the doctor if I could stay awake to watch what he was doing and he said sure.

When I got home, even though it was wintertime, I got to eat as many popsicles as I wanted, and when I went back to school a week or so later I told anyone who would listen that I was allowed to stay awake and watch the operation, and then I would open my mouth as wide as I could to show the listener that, indeed, my tonsils were gone!

I also had both kinds of measles—red and German—but the worst thing I ever caught was a bad case of mumps when I was about five. I was told many times, by anyone who saw me for the next three months or so, that I looked like a chipmunk! The mumps were on both sides of my face, and my cheeks were naturally chubby, but the mumps were also in my glands underneath my chin. I stayed in bed for what seemed like forever, with a persistent fever that would spike past 103 F. This time there was no operation and no nurse to take the night shift—just me and Mom, day after day, in my beautiful mauve-hued bedroom.

Mom would sit on my bed, and we would play endless games of Go Fish. She had filled our bathtub with cold water, and as soon as the cards became too heavy or my cheeks became red, she would throw back the covers, take off my nightie, and carry me to the bathroom for a dip in the tub to cool off. I remember being so tired I couldn't talk, or move, or protest as I was immersed in cold water. I used to hallucinate in technicolor, watching Mom's face swirl around in green and blue.

She was constantly replacing the washcloth on my forehead, and sometimes, I would see her hand coming towards me in slow motion thinking that she was reaching out to pull my hair or hit me... but all I could do was lay there, tired and hot, with a head that felt three sizes too big for my body.

In those days, doctors made house calls, and the doctor came by several times—walking into my bedroom with his big black bag to take my temperature and put his big hand on my forehead. I liked him because he had a nice smile and thought he looked so funny in that bedroom; he was so tall, he almost looked like a giant who had to duck his head when he came through the door to see a little girl lying in a big bed and her tired-looking mother—a mother who never left that room until weeks later when I could get up, step off the fluffy rug onto the cool maple floor, and walk to the bathroom on my own.

After the year of mumps, and before the year of tonsils, Mom woke up one morning feeling tingly and numb. She went to the doctor, and he said that he wanted Dad at the appointment too. After Dad arrived, the doctor told him that Mom had to take a vacation, just the two of them, where she could sleep, and eat, and drink when she wanted. She needed to relax because her "numbness" was an indication of a nervous breakdown. Dad agreed, Mom said, after some considerable yelling on the doctor's part, and Mom had to find someone to watch me while they went away for a few weeks.

Aunty Mary lived in Winnipeg. She was Mom's youngest sister. She was in her mid-thirties, was tall and thin, with cat-eye glasses and no kids, married to Uncle Sam. She said that she would come to Calgary to take care of me and to keep an eye on David, who was still living at home.

Aunty Mary had no children and liked to read all night. I hadn't started to visit Winnipeg each summer yet, so I didn't know her very well. When Mom told me that she and Dad were going on vacation and I was going to stay home with David and Aunty Mary, I had a million questions—so Mom told me all about her youngest sister Mary.

Basically, she was not a morning person, so Mom said it was unlikely that she would want to chat or sing with me in the morning. David had to be up at 2:30 a.m. to work his shift at the bakery, and I had to have some breakfast and be at school by 9 a.m., so she told me that she told David to make sure he turned the coffee pot on when he left for work.

DAVID

DAVID WAS 18, and I couldn't understand why he couldn't look after me until Mom and Dad got back. I wasn't keen on sleeping by myself because I was scared of the dark, but I thought that David should be fine to sleep with me instead of in the basement. I remember the three of us—Mom, David, and I—standing in the kitchen talking about the upcoming vacation, and Mom explaining that David couldn't sleep with me. I started to yell, "Yes!" and David would make a funny face and yell, "No!" I would stomp my foot and yell, "Yes!" and David would lower his voice and yell, "No!" Mom finally said that Aunty Mary would be arriving the day after they left, so David could sleep upstairs in their room, which was just across the hall.

After dinner that night, when it was time for me to go to bed, I started badgering David again about the sleeping arrangements. He told me that I had to sleep in my own bed and that he would sleep on the floor beside my bed on the fluffy rug. I thought that was OK, so after I gave him one of my pillows he laid down on the floor and told me to go to sleep. I told him I was not tired, and I turned over on my stomach and hung my head over the bed every once in a while to make sure he was still there. At some point I must have fallen asleep, and when I woke up it was dark, and David

39

was gone. I took a big breath and yelled "Daaaaavvvviiiddd!" and I heard him open the basement door and yell up the stairs: "Cathy, go to sleep! I'm talking to Sandy! OK? Go to SLEEP!" and I heard the door shut.

I reached down on the bedspread and had a feel around until I felt something soft and furry. Puss-Puss mewed a little as I pulled her up towards my stomach, and after a minute she settled down into a nice purr, and I guess I fell asleep. Mom and Dad were driving southwest to California, and the next day David picked up Aunty Mary from the airport and brought her back to the house on Norquay Drive.

David was the brother that was closest to me in age. He was 12 years old when I was born on a snowy Saturday morning in Misericordia Hospital in Winnipeg. Mom said that she asked both the boys if they wanted a baby sister or brother, and David said "sister." Mom said that he was young for his age, and was quite concerned that he was leaving her alone when he started school at six. He had dark hair that was long in the front and it was always combed back with something that made it shine and kept it in place.

Dad was always working, but David was at home during the day because he worked at night in the bakery and didn't go to school. He also always had a car. He'd had a rough time in school, probably some sort of learning disability or problem with attention. He used to call himself a "dumb Ukrainian" before anyone else could. He was nervous and sensitive—too sensitive for a boy living in that time with our dad.

David was always going out with his friends Johnny and Aaron to a place called the Airliner Inn, down the hill near the airport. Sometimes they didn't get home until the morning, and sometimes they slept in the car or on the front lawn. Mom said that they were drinking too much.

David used to make me cinnamon toast for breakfast. He liked sweet things, like sugar and Coke. On the days he didn't work he used to wake up early, like Mom. He never drank coffee in the morning—he always drank a bottle of Coke, and as he was usually hungover, he liked to have something to eat. He used to pull out the built-in cutting board above one of the kitchen drawers and swat away any ants that had made their way into the drawer and onto the board, get the cinnamon and butter and sugar out of the cupboard, and put the bread in the toaster.

As soon as I saw the ants I used to run around the kitchen screaming and hopping around in my bare feet, trying to avoid an ant landing on me, or stepping on one. If my cat was in the kitchen, we would try to point out the ants on the floor to see if she would eat them, but she was always uninterested in ants and would instead meow for some milk or food, which David always gave to her while saying *pssspssspsssppsss* so she would come over and see the saucer on the floor.

He liked his toast almost burned and so did I. On the mornings he made me eggs and toast, he never ate the whites, only the over-hard yolks, and so I learned to like eating the whites doused in ketchup. On the cinnamon toast mornings when the toast popped, he would put it on the cutting board, slather each slice with butter, and sprinkle cinnamon and then sugar in a thick layer, cut it in half, and hand me half a slice. He'd move me out of the way, and run down the stairs with the toast sticking out of his mouth.

David loved cars. He loved driving, *really, really* fast, and the cars he drove were all muscle cars with raised back ends, racing clutches, and not much in the way of mufflers. He used to get lots of speeding tickets—the glove box was full of them.

We drove everywhere. David was like Dad; I never saw him walk anywhere. He used to skip down the front steps and hop into the car—his hair flopping over his forehead, a cigarette hanging from his lips, in a black t-shirt, leather jacket, jeans, and cowboy boots. If he was taking me somewhere, he was always yelling for me to "Come on!"

By the time I managed to get the heavy car open, the car had already roared to life, he had revved it a few times, and if I didn't have time to shut the door properly, the forward momentum of the car acceleration did it for me.

We always drove somewhere to eat, and he always turned onto John Laurie Boulevard, as it was a wide street, a sort of straightaway. If we turned right, west towards Market Mall, we went down a steep hill with a series of curves. If we turned left, we were headed east down the hill towards the Calgary International Airport.

The car windows were never closed, and I always had to scream an answer in his direction over the sound of the engine and the radio and the wind whipping through four open windows. If he asked me a question, it was usually if I was hungry. Of course! I was always hungry! Did I want to go to Boogies or A&W? Or did I want a sundae at Dairy Queen?

I was barely tall enough to look over the bottom of the window of David's car, and when he shifted gears, slamming the clutch down and pushing the shifter from second to third (usually as he was passing someone), I remember seeing people in other cars and thinking they looked like they were moving in slow motion. David drove me around until I got a muscle car of my own when I turned 16. He showed me how much fun driving was and made me understand how driving around in a powerful car transferred that power to the driver.

I couldn't wait to get a car. Like him, I was always trying to get away from the family "situation." The yelling, the threats, the drinking, the crying, the disfunction that wasn't unique to our family but uncomfortable and scary all the same.

I think David drove like he did to get as far away from us as he could. Those drives cemented those instincts in me as well. For my entire life, if anything gets too uncomfortable emotionally, I've wanted to *run*. I have found myself running down streets, driving around in circles, or buying plane tickets to get away. Anytime we drove together, whenever I looked at him then, or remember him now... I see the same determined, haunted look on his face. I hear him saying, "Come *on*, Cathy! Let's *go*!"

DAVID AND PATTY AND SANDY

DAVID LOVED A girl named Sandy, who was always in the car, but Mom said that Sandy's parents didn't think that David was "good enough" to marry their daughter.

Soon after, a different girl—named Patty—was in the car. And as far as girlfriends go, I liked Patty better than Sandy. She used to talk to me and hug me and bring me little presents. Patty and David got married when I was eight or nine. After Patty got pregnant, David still had a muscle car, a metallic dull green 1967 Camaro with a manual transmission. Patty wasn't very tall, so when she took me somewhere in the car, she would have to sit on a phone book and wear big wedgie shoes to push the clutch in to get it started.

One night I heard crying and yelling in the kitchen. I got out of bed and walked down the hall to the brightly lit kitchen. David was pacing around yelling, and Patty and Mom were sitting and talking. Patty was crying, and her hair was all messed up, and her stockings were torn at the knee, and she had blood on her leg. I walked over to her, and she gave me a hug, and when Mom saw me she told me to go back to bed. But I stayed there for a while, leaning against Patty, picking at the hole in her stockings, asking her if I should get her a band aid. Mom was telling David to keep his voice

43

down, but he kept pacing back and forth with his finger stuck in his mouth, chewing on his nails. His eyes were very bright and the whole kitchen smelled like beer.

Patty and David had had an argument and Patty had wanted to get out of the car, but David didn't stop the car completely, and Patty had fallen out into the street. Mom told me to go back to bed, that everything was fine, and Patty hugged me and said that she was sorry she had woken me up.

I came home from school every day for lunch. One day I walked up the stairs and Mom was sitting in one of the chairs in the living room crying. She said that David had been hurt and had lots of stitches in his face and had nearly lost his eye. He had been out all night, and when Patty came over she saw Sandy's sweater in David's car. David was in the backyard, lying on a lawn chair in the sun, sleeping—so Patty walked upstairs and filled one of our big clear water glasses with a heavy base, and walked around the side of the house to throw some water on him to wake him up. The glass slipped out of her hand when she threw the water, so she ran around the side of the house to the front, thinking he was going to chase her—but he didn't. She walked back to the backyard to see that the glass had landed on his face and shattered, and his face was a bloody mess, and he had been knocked out. Mom had taken him and Patty to the ER to get David's face stitched up. Patty said it was an accident. She had just wanted to know why he had Sandy's sweater in his car.

One Saturday, Patty called around suppertime to say that David had come home and was acting insane. He had been out all day with friends, likely drinking and taking drugs. He was yelling and screaming and had started to throw some of their furniture off the third-floor balcony. Dad asked if I wanted to come, and I said sure. I thought that maybe Patty needed my help, so we drove over to the apartment and saw a bunch of furniture and stuff on the lawn. We could hear David yelling and headed up the stairs. I walked into the bedroom where Patty was lying on the bed crying, and Dad went into the living room to try to talk to David.

A few minutes later someone knocked on the door, and when I answered it, there were two policemen asking about the disturbance. David started to yell at them, and the police asked Dad and Patty and I to come out into the hall so they could go inside to talk to David. They did, and then they came out in the hall to say that David wasn't cooperating, and they might have to arrest him. Dad told David that if he stayed in the apartment and stopped yelling and throwing things off the balcony, the police wouldn't arrest him.

David walked out into the hall, and the police handcuffed him and took him to the police station. Dad kept saying that he should have just stayed in the apartment, but David never listened to anyone.

THE CAR

ONE MORNING, WHEN Mom and Dad were away on their vacation and Aunty Mary was looking after David and me, we woke up to a foot of snow that had fallen overnight. I normally walked to school, but it was a blizzard, so Aunty Mary said that after breakfast she would drive me to school. Aunty Mary wasn't used to going out in the morning but the school was down the hill only a few blocks away so still in her nightgown, she slipped on one of Mom's fur coats and a pair of David's cowboy boots, and we walked through the backyard to the garage.

The Yurkiw car was a big, heavy, low, 1967 Cadillac Brougham, and although Aunty Mary was used to driving a big car, the snow was deep. We made it down the alley to the bottom of the hill, and pulled up in front of the school, but the car—with a half-dressed, sleepy Aunty Mary in it—got stuck. I told Aunty Mary that one of my best friends' dads had a garage just a little further down the hill, and he could probably help. One of the other parents walked into the school and called Hilland's garage. When Alan Hilland arrived in the tow truck, he introduced himself as Barbara's dad, and Aunty Mary got out of the car to hug him.

I waved goodbye to Aunty Mary, and turned back a couple of times to make sure she was doing OK with the car. She was standing there in the wind and the snow, trying to hold Mom's fur coat closed over her knee-length threadbare nightie, with her light thin hair flying around her hatless head. I could hear her telling Mr. Hilland who she was and where she was from and why she was dressed that way—she had been up late talking to David and never got up this early—as he walked her over to the tow truck so she could keep warm in the cab while he hooked up the Cadillac and towed it back up the hill. It didn't look to me like Mr. Hilland managed to get a word in edgewise while he was trying to steer her towards the truck, as she hung onto his arm with one hand and held her coat closed with the other. When I got home at three, all the snow had melted, and the car was back in the garage at the house on Norquay Drive.

David and Dad did not get along. David and Richard both moved out shortly before they got married, a year or so apart in the early 1970s—though they continued to work for him at the bakery. One night, the police came to the door because David had gotten into a car accident on his way to work. He was going down the hill on 14th St. at 2:15 in the morning and a car ran a red light on 16th Avenue and hit him.

Dad went to the hospital, and Mom stayed home with me. David was a little banged up, especially one of his knees because the front end of the car had been nearly torn off, and part of the engine had come down onto his knees. Dad told him that it served him right for speeding, but David insisted that the other guy had run the red light and David had tried to stop.

A few days after David got out of the hospital, Dad told me that we were going to the wrecking yard where David's car had been towed. The car was a twisted hunk of metal, and all of us walked around the car trying to identify it for sure as David's GTO. David said that Dad had to believe him about trying to stop and not hit the guy who had run the red light. He hobbled over to what he thought was the front of the car the car on his crutches, and told Dad to come and take a look. Both of David's cowboy boots were still sitting on top of the brake pedal, just like his legs were still inside, with one of them covered in blood.

David had been trapped and bleeding in the car, waiting for the cops and the ambulance to come and pull him out. Dad lifted me up so I could see, and I thought the blood on the cowboy boots was kind of gross, and David kept saying, "See? See?" to Dad, who finally muttered something like "Well, you were probably *both* speeding, or he wouldn't have hit you so hard." And David just smirked and hobbled back to our car on his crutches.

The guy driving the car that ran the red light that night, who hit David's car, had just kept going—until a few blocks down 16th Avenue, his car stopped because one of his front tires had been nearly torn off in the collision. The guy jumped out of his car and tried to run, but he was so drunk he just fell onto the sidewalk and the cops picked him up at the scene. He didn't have a scratch on him.

RICHARD

RICHARD WASN'T AT home very often. He shared a room downstairs with David, but they used to fight all the time, and Richard and Dad didn't get along. Richard was two years older than David, but he always acted much older. He was always going in and out of the house, brushing past me as he went.

He had a couple of girlfriends I liked, especially Norma, who had red hair, and gave me a music box that had a ballerina that spun around to music when I lifted the lid. I used to wind it up and make Barbie dance a little jig, along with the ballerina in the box.

Mom said that Richard was learning to be a cake decorator… that was his job at the bakery, and he was always practicing. I used to take a big slab cake to school on special occasions like Valentine's Day or St. Patrick's Day because Richard needed to practice… and Dad probably thought giving a free cake to my school class was great marketing!

Needless to say, these cakes were a big hit with my classmates, and on cake days I used to get a ride to school in the white bakery van. I would kneel in the back, holding onto the cake, while we made our way down the hill to the school. Walking with Richard—who was holding the cake—down the long hall to my classroom was about the only time we did anything together, except when we started going to Montana.

Richard used to race speedboats, and he had a blue truck with a camper on the back, and he was always going to races—sometimes all the way to Montana. I remember lying on the top bunk in the camper looking out the rectangular window, while we flew down the highway pulling his boat. When we got to whatever lake he was racing on we would park at a campground, and at night there would be a campfire and a whole bunch of his friends, who were competing or were there to cheer him on. There was always lots of laughing and joking and beer and food, and although he didn't really talk to me any more than he did at home, he seemed happier and more relaxed.

Richard married a girl named Heather, who was the daughter of a woman who worked at Dad's bakery in Forest Lawn. Heather's family was Scottish, so they went to Scotland on their honeymoon. They had two very exotic-looking Siamese cats, which they dropped off at our house to look after while they were away. We kept them in the basement and once Puss-Puss came down the stairs, probably smelling a feline intruder or intruders, took one look at them, hissed, and stalked off. I loved cats, so I was always trying to get them to come out of their basement hiding place so I could play with them.

At that time, I also had a couple of budgies I named Bonnie and Clyde (the budgie-budgie bank robbers) one of which was blue and the other green. They lived in a cage in Dad's office, also downstairs.

One day I got so frustrated that Richard's cats wouldn't come out to play with me that I opened the door to Dad's office, where Bonnie and Clyde were happily chirping away, and I opened their cage door a little bit, hoping that Richard's cats would come over to see who was chirping—but then I got bored, and went down the hall to watch TV. By the time I heard wild chirping, and the cage being knocked over by the bloodthirsty Siamese twin cats, the deed was done. Bonnie and Clyde were no more. Just a few feathers on the floor...

THE WINTER CLUB WEDDINGS

RICHARD AND DAVID both got married at the Calgary Winter Club, and as Dad was in business, the weddings were *huge*, with 300+ people attending. There was a lot of pre-wedding activities, and I attended two events that were very different.

Richard was marrying Heather, who didn't care for me at all. After sweet Norma, I was sort of disappointed when this girl saw me as a rival—she used to pinch my arm whenever Richard wasn't looking, especially when we drove somewhere together, and I would wiggle my way in between them, sitting on the big front bench seat in Richard's white convertible.

Richard and Heather had bought a small house in southwest Calgary, and one night a few months before the wedding they had an engagement party. The house was much smaller than ours, and it was filled with people. I had received an autograph book for Christmas, and as I didn't think I was going to run into any celebrities in North Haven, I brought it along to see if some of the people at the party would sign it.

When Mom dropped me off, I saw that David was mixing drinks at the bar, and Sandy was there. So were David's friends Aaron and Johnny, and Richard's friend Keith who's family owned the Phillips

66 station near the Dairy Queen on 14th Street at the corner of John Laurie Boulevard. Lots of people at the party knew who I was, as Richard always told everyone that I was his "kid sister," and I remember I got lots and lots of autographs for my book. The music was loud, and everyone was having a good time. Someone had a Polaroid camera and was taking pictures.

I still have some of those pictures, and one day I'll put them in a frame and explain to people what my brother's engagement party looked like in Calgary in 1969.

A few years later, David married Patty, and before the wedding we went to a fondue party at Patty's mom and dad's house to celebrate their engagement. I remember Patty's parents' house was not too far from ours, and we probably could have walked, but of course we drove. I had no idea what fondue was, but Mom had received the invitation in the mail, and had put it on the long table in the dining room, and I must have looked at it a million times, trying to imagine how we were all going to *fondue*!

When the big night came, we were ushered into the living room and all the furniture was gone, and there was a low long table sitting almost on the shag-carpeted floor, with cushions all around the table. The table had four strange looking small pots sitting on wire contraptions, with what looked like a little candle underneath each one. I could smell something cooking, and it smelled pretty good! All around the pots were platters filled with tiny slices of fruit and vegetables and meat, and at each cushion there was a small plate with a strange looking fork-thing that had either a yellow, orange, or green plastic handle.

The adults were all in the kitchen getting drinks, and I went over to Dad to tell him that we were going to have to *sit on the floor* and eat *vegetables* using *little forks*, and even though he had his company smile on, he looked at me and said, "Cathy, don't be crazy." Still smiling, he shoved me out of the kitchen.

It was a good thing I was wearing pants, but I had no idea how Mom was going to sit and eat in her knee-length dress. Dad sitting cross-legged at a low table was something I couldn't even imagine. And as I saw no pork chops, steak, or pan-fried potatoes on that table, I had no idea what he was going to eat.

SUNSHINE GIRL

I WAS INCLUDED in Richard's wedding party as a flower girl. The wedding was a production, and endless preparations were needed. I was told one day that we were going dress shopping with Heather and her bridesmaids, and that it would be fun because I was getting a special flower girl dress to wear for the wedding. As a chubby six-year-old who wore as few clothes and shoes as I could get away with, the idea of wearing what my mother described as "a long satin dress" filled me with dread.

The wedding dress store was full of giggling girls, and after what seemed like days, the bridesmaid dresses were chosen, and so were the flower girl dresses—I was one of two flower girls, and clearly the other girl was more excited than I was. The wedding day came and went, and after posing for a million pictures that I am mostly scowling in—Mom used to call it "the Sam Yurkiw look"—the festivities were over. By the end of the night I didn't quite hate the hot, scratchy, dress as much as at the start of the day.

A month or so later it was announced that our school would be putting on a play. Everyone was welcome to audition, and the parts were passed out for everyone to read and consider what part you were interested in trying out for. One particular part was of interest to me, and one morning the announcements included a list of which students had been chosen for what part. I was shocked to hear my name announced, and received my script to begin memorizing for the big night. My across the street neighbor, one of a set of twins, was named as my counterpart at what was to be the conclusion of the play. We spent many an afternoon outside—sitting on our respective front porches, or down by the lamp post where we skipped double Dutch—reciting our lines. My flower girl dress became my costume, and I was never sure if I was chosen for the part because of the dress, and its beautiful shade of harvest not quite gold.

The night of the play was a triumph, with multiple standing ovations; as I was wheeled out on a sort of wagon type of vehicle to the strains of the Beatles hit "Here Comes The Sun," my neighbor Debbie entered the stage shortly after on a similar vehicle complete with a huge silver crescent moon accompanied by Andy Williams crooning "Moon River." As we were wheeled past each other as our respective songs played, we smiled while waving to the adoring crowd of parents, like two future beauty queens that were never to be.

But for one night, Debbie and I were the queens of the fourth grade North Haven Elementary school play.

DAD

DAD LOVED TO drive. It was the only thing he loved more than work, and Sunday mornings he and I usually had breakfast at Phil's Pancake House. I always had the same thing: scrambled eggs and silver dollar pancakes with a side of sausage links. And every Sunday morning he would tease his chubby six-year-old daughter who could only manage to eat two sausage links. Didn't I know how much extra he had paid for those?

Every couple of months we drove to the Phil's in Banff, and I usually fell asleep in the car, waking to the sweet smell of the air in the mountains. Sometimes I would fall asleep on the way to Banff and wake up after Dad had parked the car, and he and Mom had gone into the restaurant and ordered coffee. Mom said that they always sat at a booth near the window so they could see the locked car with me sleeping in the back seat. A couple of times I woke up hungry and crabby in an empty car and started to cry as Mom made her way out of the restaurant to rescue me.

After breakfast we would drive around or head over to the Gondola, where Mom would walk around while Dad and I rode to the top. The view up there was something I never forgot, no matter how many years I lived somewhere else. The sound—or lack of sound—always amazed me. Like you were standing in a room with no air, it was so still and quiet, and from the observation platform, you actually looked down on the beautiful, majestic, snow-capped Rocky Mountains.

Dad regularly picked up a hitchhiker on the way back to Calgary. No hippies, mind you; he liked to pick up clean-cut kids who looked like he wished my brothers would. Short hair, neat clothes, carrying a backpack. Sitting in the back seat with a stranger didn't seem too odd. Mom and Dad did the chatting while I read my Archie comic.

Dad had a couple of bakeries. He had an office downstairs in the house where the boys slept. He worked all the time. Early morning to late at night and on the weekends. I used to go with him to the bakery in Forest Lawn on the weekends, usually after we had gone to Phil's Pancake House for breakfast. Mom said every morning after breakfast, I would slam the car door and stomp up the front steps to the blue door with the screen to complain that he was teasing me about the cost of the sausages. Mom said that Dad didn't know what to do with me. He didn't know why what he said bothered me. He thought I was funny.

He did things with me he never did with the boys. He taught me to skate at the Winter Club. He used to push me over and tell me to get up, as that was the hardest part of skating. He used to take me driving and to Stampede. When we went on car trips to Disneyland or Las Vegas, I used to sit in the front seat with him while Mom slept in the back. We used to talk about where we were going and about the scenery.

When he would get tired or Mom would insist, he would stop at a diner, and he always wanted to taste the pie. He loved gross pies like raisin or cherry. I loved apple pie, with ice cream. Mom never ate pie; she just drank black coffee and smoked, watching us eat and critique the pie.

Calgary was all about my dad. He would take me to the bakery in Forest Lawn, while he did some work, and I put together boxes for cakes and stuffed my face with frozen chocolate cupcakes (no icing, of course). One time, Dad took David's car—a sporty car, a Camaro, or the blue GTO—and we drove downtown. He stalled it in an intersection, and I remember the streets were almost deserted, and the buildings were tall, and we drove right underneath the Husky Tower. I felt super special, just me and my dad cruising around in downtown Calgary in a sportscar.

SPY HILL JAIL

EVENTUALLY, THE UNPAID speeding tickets David kept stuffed in his glovebox led to a summons, which led to a suspension of his driver's license, and him driving anyway... and somehow, unbelievably, my 19-year-old "dumb Ukrainian" smart-ass of a brother ended up incarcerated at the newly constructed Spy Hill Jail.

I don't know how long he was in there. Mom never said anything to me, and I have no idea how I found out, but for a while after I figured out what jail was, I told all the kids I played with in the neighborhood that my brother had gone there. Sometimes, I faced Nose Hill, and pointed dramatically, so they would understand that I knew where the jail was located, and that my brother had broken the law and had ended up in there.

The truth was, I didn't have a clue about suspended driving licenses, DUIs, consequences of not paying your speeding tickets, or even how many speeding tickets a 19-year-old boy could accumulate before he got thrown in jail. All I knew was that Mom was either crying or yelling or silent, and the thought of her son even spending one night in jail was the worst thing that had happened to us as a family so far.

I don't remember what happened when David got out of jail—how he was, if he had changed—but it was like he disappeared after that. We didn't drive together as much, he wasn't home as much, and he seemed to be very short-tempered. Sometimes I would ask him something, and he would spin around and yell at me. That had never happened before. He was really jumpy and impatient, and he was constantly pushing me out of the way, like he couldn't even look at me. One day I came home from school, and there was a hole in the drywall in the dining room. It looked like someone had punched it. I asked Mom about it, but all she said was that David banged into it by accident.

Things seemed to be changing, and not just at home…

Things Going Wrong

BARBARA HILLAND WAS a few years older than me, and her brothers were very close in age to David and Richard. Like my brothers, they worked for their dad. I always thought that the Hillands were a perfect family—kind, quiet, and polite. Everything at Barbara's house was so nice and... normal.

But one day we were in the playroom listening to some records and heard the front door slam. One of Barbara's brothers had come in, with Barbara's dad right behind him. *Slam! Slam!* Then we heard yelling, and all of a sudden furniture being knocked over, and more yelling, and Barbara started to cry.

She turned up the volume on the record player and took my hand and led me into the corner of the room, both of us standing staring at the closed door. After a bit more yelling, the front door slammed again, and all of a sudden Barbara's dad flung open the door and yelled at Barbara to turn down the music. He was all red in the face, with his hair messed up, and he glared at the two of us and slammed the door.

I went over and turned down the music, my heart pounding, and Barbara found a Kleenex and blew her nose. We just stared at each other, and she said that I should go home. I stood by the door, not knowing if I should open it or not, but when I didn't hear anything except someone walking upstairs to the bedrooms I pulled open the door, tiptoed down the short hallway to the front door, and let myself out.

I started to feel a little dizzy as I walked down the stairs and realized I had been holding my breath.

Once, I woke up late at night to Mom standing in the living room looking out the picture window through the sheer curtains. The entire living room was bathed in red, white, and blue flashing lights from the police cars and ambulance outside. Dad had walked down the stairs to the front door after someone rang the doorbell, and a Calgary Police officer introduced himself. When the police officer saw me standing at the top of the stairs, he asked Dad if he could step outside and answer a few questions, so Dad went outside and closed the door behind him.

I walked over to where Mom was standing and asked if something had happened to David. She put her arm around my shoulder and squeezed me close to her legs and said that David was out with Aaron and Johnny, but that there had been an accident across the street. Dad came in after about 10 minutes and told Mom in a quiet voice what the policemen had said had happened.

I sort of knew the boy who lived across the street. He was a little older than I was. He had an older brother who wasn't as old as David and Richard but was maybe 16 or 17. There was a gun in their basement that was supposed to be locked up, but somehow the boy my age had gotten it out and was playing with it. The boy's parents were out.

When his older brother came downstairs and saw that he had the gun, he tried to take it away from him. The younger boy didn't want his older brother to have it, so there was a struggle. When the gun went off, the older boy was holding the gun, and suddenly the younger boy was lying on the floor bleeding.

The older brother called an ambulance, and the ambulance dispatcher called the police, and as we stood watching, the boy's parents pulled up and started running down the street towards their house while the ambulance people wheeled out a stretcher with a sheet pulled over the younger boy's face. The older brother was being escorted down the sidewalk crying and handcuffed, being put into the back of a police car by two grim-faced City of Calgary Police officers.

The boys' mother was calling their names over and over while she ran towards the ambulance, and Mom looked at Dad and said that she was going to get dressed and go over to see if there was anything she could do. She squeezed his arm and told him to put me back to bed.

Baba Was Everything

I HAD A Baba. And no matter where I lived, she and Grampa—I had problems pronouncing Gido—used to get on a plane and come and visit.

Baba looked at me like I was something good to eat. In broken English she would ask me how school was, and she used to give me a five-dollar bill and tell me to hide it! (After Baba died, my mom told me how she and her sisters had found close to a thousand dollars sewn into Baba's underwear!)

When she unzipped her suitcase, among the clothes was a ring of garlic sausage, a loaf of bread from Kub bakery, and some Rosebuds.

In my mind, she lived faraway, and because Baba was old, the journey was hard—but she had done it just to see me.

By the time I was six, my mom was exhausted. She had had a hysterectomy that in those days required a huge incision and a hospital stay. She had two teenage boys, one who started drinking at 14, a workaholic, cheating husband and what they used to refer to as "nerves." Mom needed a break, so I started flying to Winnipeg each summer just after Stampede. My mom would hand me over to someone at the Air Canada counter, and they would walk me onto the plane, sit me in the front row, and I would drink my juice

69

while resting my head on the small plastic plane window, staring down at the flat patchwork of yellows and greens that made up the Canadian prairies.

I never knew who was going to be waiting for me at the Winnipeg airport. As I stepped onto the escalator going down into the arrivals area, I would scan the crowd and wave to Uncle Thor or Aunty Mary.

On the familiar car ride from the airport to Baba's house—*always* my first stop—I could imagine her in her small backyard garden filled with dill that was taller than I was, and lower down, lettuce and radishes. There was always clean, fresh laundry hanging on the line. I loved the smell and the sound of the *snap* as the clothes whipped back and forth in the wind.

I used to help Baba put the dry clothes in the laundry basket as she stood on the little wooden platform, unpinning each piece as the plastic-covered line squeaked on the rusty metal pulley. One by one, she would drop the clothes on my head, and we would both laugh.

As soon as the car came to a stop in the back alley next to the garage, I would jump out and run down the sidewalk to the left of the duplex. Baba was watching out of the kitchen window that faced the alley, and she knew when I had arrived. I could see the screen door swing open, and before a word was spoken, I was gathered up like a pile of wet laundry into the arms of this big soft woman who smelled like face powder, yeasty dough, and mothballs. She always had on a flowered dress and an apron, and even on a humid July day, thick flesh-colored stockings and shoes. When she was finished hugging me, she always said the same thing: "Cathy, you're so *skinny!*" and would spin me around and lead me up the three stairs from the landing into her kitchen.

I can still see every detail of that kitchen. The small window over the sink, and the bigger window to the right above the tiny little red Formica table and chairs. The cupboards were plain light wood with big flat wooden knobs. On the left there was a small shelf open to Baba's bedroom with a curvaceous black Bakelite phone with a funny number—JU67067. The phone, unlike our modern one at home, was a party line, and sometimes I would pick it up and hear conversations.

The kitchen is where I remember Baba the most. I could smell food as soon as I walked in the door, and it always smelled so much better than any food we ever ate at our house. She'd sit me down at the kitchen table and ask me questions, half in English, half in Ukrainian. "Is your mom drinking? How is David?" I would try to explain, while one by one, plates appeared on the table. Perogies, homemade chicken soup with homemade noodles, borscht, or cabbage rolls. It didn't matter. I loved them all.

In the hour or so it would take me to eat as much food as I could, my extended family would trickle in. They all spoke Ukrainian, and I would try to work out what was being said, but Baba would just smile at me while she spoke to them. The feeling I got in that kitchen was like a warm hug, and if I could have spent my entire visit in that shiny red and chrome chair, I would have been perfectly happy.

I followed Baba around like a puppy. Everything she did seemed like fun. From picking dill in the garden to washing clothes downstairs in the basement with an old wringer washer.

Every other day we walked down the street for soft ice cream, and on the way back she used to point to the big high school across the street, and whisper that if I would come and live with her in Winnipeg I could go to school there!

I slept with her, and she would tell me stories about the old country. Exciting stories about hiding under beds and in stacks of hay, and of bad men, and then she would hug me and tell me to go to sleep.

The living room had an old-fashioned S-shaped green sectional sofa, a big radio, and a small TV so Grandpa could watch wrestling. We used to sit on the sofa and look at old photo albums that sat on a high shelf in a front hall closet that held Baba's fur coats. While Baba was getting the albums, I always took a minute to give the long fur coats with the shiny satin lining a squeeze and a sniff.

The black and white photos were mounted on black pages and were mostly of people I didn't know. Baba would explain who was who, but most of the people lived in the old country or they knew them from the farm. I just liked to sit there and listen to her describe how these individuals were or were not related to me.

I remember one photo of Baba and Grampa standing in a plowed field beside a man—Baba's brother, I think. Baba had on a flowered babushka, and she and Grampa looked so stiff in the picture, like they were posing for a wedding photo, not in a field somewhere in Ukraine.

Baba and Grampa traveled back to Ukraine a few times. She brought me a babushka, and a fine white shirt embroidered in black and red flowers. She bought a pair of rose gold earrings on one visit, and when she showed them to me, she whispered that when she died I was supposed to take them out of her ears because they would belong to me.

My aunts and uncles would arrive on and off during the three or four days I spent with Baba, and in Ukrainian the negotiations would begin. Where I would go next? With who? And for how long?

A House in a
Different Decade

BABA AND GRAMPA lived in a duplex. Not a side-by-side… an up and down split with two doors in the front. We always used the side door to get into Baba and Grampa's, but Sonny and Carol lived upstairs. Sonny's real name was William or Bill… and he was Baba and Grandpa's oldest son, my mom's brother. As it was in those days, Baba had been pregnant at Mom's wedding, so Sonny and Mom had never lived in the same house, and like David and Richard and me, there was a significant age gap. Sonny was 19 years younger than my mom, and Baba would have her last child—another boy, named Russell—2 years later. Mom said that when Bill was born he was sooooo cute, with white-blonde hair and blue eyes. The sisters thought he looked just like the little boy on the Sunny Boy Cereal box, so everyone called him Sonny.

Sonny was an artist. He was in Art School, and made silk-screened prints, not paintings. He was married to a beautiful blonde woman named Carol, who wore big glasses, and had a beautiful smile and spoke in a quiet little girl voice.

Walking up the stairs to Sonny and Carol's was like stepping into a different decade. The footprint of the apartment was a mirror

73

image of downstairs, but it couldn't have been more different. Every single wall was painted a different color—cantaloupe orange, aqua blue, lemon yellow, and mossy green, with big bright art pieces on each wall. Sometimes the pictures were in frames, and sometimes put up with thumb tacks.

Sonny and Carol had very little furniture, and instead of a couch, they had big cushions on the floor, in multicolor printed batik-type fabrics. It was so beautiful and bright and fresh, especially compared to Baba and Grampa's place that looked like a black and white film set in the 1940s. Carol even had two Siamese cats who lolled on the pillows, lazily meowing and squeaking when they saw me and then going back to sleep.

Baba had a dog named Brutus, who was *her* dog, and she only spoke to him in Ukrainian, and he did whatever she wanted him to. Carol's cats sometimes came down to the basement where Baba's washing machine was, and she would hiss and shoo them away because clearly Baba was a dog person… and she didn't believe that animals belonged in the house.

Sonny and Carol's friends were all artists, and Aunty Mary loved to support her brother by going to openings, sometimes at Sonny's studio, the Grand Western Canadian Screen Shop. I don't think Baba thought that artist was something that Sonny should be. However, I have a framed picture, a photocopy of a piece that Sonny told me he did in the style of the Group of Seven especially for Baba, so she could show her friends and understand that Sonny was not just a screen printer but a painter… you know, like a *real* artist.

I was in awe of Sonny and Carol…they were so different from David and Richard and the rest of my family. I was too young to spend a lot of time with them, but that apartment made a huge impression on me.

THE HOUSE ON LINDSAY

MY FIRST STOP after Baba's was usually Aunty Mary's house. She lived on a nice quiet street with a huge weeping willow tree in the front yard. Her house was filled to the brim with furniture, antiques, art, and books. She had a nice old fat cat, a sweet tabby (also named Puss-Puss) and usually at least one dog. Her husband was my Uncle Sam, a chubby, smiling man who always seemed glad to see me. Mary and Sam owned Winnipeg Lock and Key, so on the days Mary had to work, she would take me to the "shop" on Notre Dame Avenue and we would always make Uncle Sam take us out for lunch at the Greek restaurant around the corner.

Aunty Mary was tall and thin, and reminded me of a spider. She didn't walk, she slinked along, usually in some sort of multicolored, flowy outfit that looked great on her. She always had incredible jewelry, a gold charm bracelet dripping with charms, and a gold rope of a necklace with a Mabe pearl the size of my chubby hand.

When Aunty Mary entered a room, people turned around to look. She had a low raspy voice, and a dirty laugh. When she greeted the man who owned the restaurant, she didn't walk over to him, she curled herself around him like a snake, or a skinny cat with a long tail… it was like she flowed right through people.

Aunty Mary always wore high heels, and her natural height combined with the heels created an illusion of height that made me feel like a chubby little dwarf, barely reaching her thigh. She always introduced me as her niece from Calgary, like I had traveled a million miles to see her, and I could see the people looking at me—thinking, *really, this chubby little thing in the stained t-shirt and the rumpled pants and the dirty sneakers? Mary's niece? How odd...*

Mary did the books at the shop, and after lunch, she probably did an hour or so of work, then talked to people for about an hour on the phone while I hung around. When it was time to go she always gathered her enormous purse and her even bigger keychain loaded with keys. The sound of the keys together with the charm bracelet caused Mary to jingle all the way to her huge car! Our next stop was the grocery store and then home to make dinner.

I used to sleep in the back bedroom, with Puss-Puss, and the bed had about five old quilts on it. The warm brass of the bed, mixed with the quilts and the cat, made for a cozy nest for a few nights, as we always split our time between that house and Mary and Sam's cabin on Bird Lake. The drive was a couple of hours, and Aunty Mary would keep me entertained with stories about her friends, Uncle Sam, and Aunty Nancy, so the time flew by.

When we got to the cabin, we had to carry the groceries from the car down the path to the front door, and then get the beds made depending on who was joining us. We always had popcorn and played scrabble and read and talked... and if Uncle Sam was on his way after work, or in a day or two, I knew that we would be going fishing for jackfish (which you couldn't eat) or pickerel or trout (which you could).

Uncle Sam would wake me up between three and four in the morning, and we would head down the path to the dock and the boat. Once I was in my lifejacket, he would start the engine by pulling a string, and we would be off, somewhere where the fish would be biting. We'd stay there for hours, and he used to ask me questions about Mom and Dad or school, and a couple of times in the next couple of hours, one of us would feel a jiggle on the lines and Uncle Sam would spring into action to make sure we caught whatever fish had taken our bait.

We usually came back to the cabin with something, and he would filet the fish and fry it up, make some coffee on the stove, and make me beer pancakes with lots of butter and syrup. Aunty Mary would sleep through our breakfasts, as she was definitely not a morning person, but whenever she woke up, Uncle Sam would launch into a story about our exciting morning of fishing, and by that time (full of fish and pancakes), I would lie down on the couch in the living room for a nap.

My Godfather Thor, Aunty Nancy, and Berniece

AFTER A FEW days at the lake, it was time to go back to Winnipeg, and Aunty Mary would drop me off at Aunty Nancy's for the afternoon. Uncle Sam was a lot of fun, but Uncle Thor, who was married to Aunty Nancy, was my godfather and visiting with him at work was a lot more fun.

Aunty Nancy was the sister closest in age to my mom, and they were both born in the old country. I thought she was funny and outrageous. She was a mean drunk (although not when I visited), and of all the sisters, she was the one who never went to AA. She made my cousin Patty's life a living hell. A mother she wasn't, nor a cook, nor a particularly good wife. She was a liar in a style that could be described as "colorful," or "vicious."

I never knew any of this growing up... it was all hinted at. I saw Aunty Nancy as someone who paid very little attention to you unless she thought you could be useful in some way, and at my age, with my cheerful nature, I was of no use to her. Like my mother... too sweet, no guts... no fun to tease... a *noonka*, in Ukrainian.

Aunty Nancy worked from home: she used to cold call people from a list to ask them if they would like to have their furnace cleaned. To hear Aunty Nancy on the phone, you would think she was the sweetest, nicest woman on the planet, but it was all an act.

After a morning of phone calls, Aunty Nancy would ask me if I wanted a baloney sandwich or a can of soup, and then she would flop down on the couch to watch *General Hospital*.

They had a cat I had only seen a few times. She was as gray as sooty ash, with big green eyes, and plush fur that looked like velvet, but I had only seen her running in the opposite direction.

Aunty Nancy said she would call Bernice for me, and as I was sitting on the floor I thought I had a good chance of seeing her for the first time, up close. Aunty Nancy threw back her head, and started to call in a sing-song voice.

"Berrrrnneeiiceeee... It's *General Hospital* Time... Berrrrnnneeiice... *pssssspssspssss.*"

I was asked to turn the TV on to channel whatever, and as I took my place, on the floor, right near the couch, I waited for the phantom cat to arrive. Aunty Nancy said she was probably in the basement and was coming.

Sure enough, I heard the basement door slowly creak open, and this gorgeous gray cat with sleepy eyes meowed quietly when she entered the living room to announce that she had arrived and was ready to watch *General Hospital*. Then, suddenly, she stopped, and her eyes opened so wide I thought she was going to attack me. She looked straight at me, and as I was reaching out my hand to possibly touch her head, *vroooom!* Just like in the cartoons. Nothing but a puff of imaginary smoke where a pretty cat should have been... Bernice had streaked out of the room, *never* to be seen by me again.

Aunty Nancy took her eyes off the screen for a minute and poked me in the shoulder and asked me why I had scared poor Bernice. She suggested I go down to the basement and look for her, but I was frozen in place, worried that Bernice wasn't a real cat but some kind of wild-cat-creature that would finish me off if I stepped onto the basement stairs.

Aunty Nancy said that after *General Hospital* she was going to take me to see Uncle Thor. An hour later, we were walking down the street to the bus stop.

Uncle Thor had driven a bus for Winnipeg Transit for 40 years. He had a beautiful smile, and a gray brush cut, and a laugh that sounded like a train was chugging past. When the bus stopped, Aunty Nancy said goodbye, and Uncle Thor said hello and told me to sit in the front seat so he could talk to me and drive at the same time. He asked me about school and Mom and Dad and how the weather was in Calgary and did I win any prizes at Stampede?

Mom *loved* Uncle Thor, and I guess that's why she chose him to be my godfather, along with an old friend of hers, Olga Walco. I never saw Olga… not sure where she lived, but Uncle Thor and I were friends. He told me about the Bus Drivers Union and something called the NDP that kept the union strong. We talked about the Winnipeg Blue Bombers and the quarterback who was good last year, but wasn't good for nothin' this year—he used to go to football games with Uncle Sam in the outdoor arena in the winter! As we drove around, he told me that he was glad that I was such a nice girl, not like the brats he sometimes had on the bus, snooty rich kids who went to school in River Heights. He said that he would drop me off near Aunty Mary's house in River Heights, and he was off the next day, and he would take me downtown to Kelekis's restaurant on Main Street for a hotdog if I wanted to go.

I said sure, and he said we were coming up to the Lindsay Street stop. The bus stopped, and he put it in park, and he rifled around in his jacket for a bundle of colored pencils and walked me down onto the sidewalk. He asked me if I knew where I was, and I nodded yes, and he asked me to point where Aunty Mary's house was, and what her house number was. I told him, and he said that was right, and he handed me the pencils and gave me a hug and told me to start walking. I turned around and waved, and he was standing on the sidewalk and he waved back and he yelled that he would pick me up tomorrow.

SUMMERS AT THE DEVIL'S INN

BABA AND GRAMPA had a cottage at Grand Beach called "The Devil's Inn," and I loved to go there. It had no running water: we used to walk to the end of the lane and pump water into a bucket and take it back to the kitchen.

There was an outhouse, which was too dark and scary and smelly for me, or public bathrooms at the end of the same lane. In those public bathrooms, when the fish flies were thick on the walls, I used to scream at the top of my lungs because I was convinced they were going to attack me... and because I loved the echo. When I came out of the stall, Baba would be standing there talking to the other old ladies and laughing.

The cottage had three bedrooms, with three quarter beds and curtains for doors. The floor was linoleum tile, nice and cool on sandy wet feet at the end of a day spent at the beach. The living room had an old couch and chair, both covered with blankets. The only decoration was a big painting in the wall above the sofa that was all swirly greens and whites. That painting used to scare me as a kid, as I thought the picture also sometimes had eyes, especially at night when whoever I had been sleeping with, Baba, or Aunty Mary, or Aunty Nancy, would help me get out of bed so I could go out in the backyard to have a pee.

I remember how warm and light the cottage was at night, except on thunderstorm nights when everyone would be inside—playing a game, or talking, or drinking beer—and I would be running around in the backyard, screaming every time I saw lightning in the sky or heard a big clap of thunder.

The kitchen was the entire length of the cottage at the back, and Baba used to stand at the sink washing vegetables or doing dishes so she could watch me, and after a particularly blood curdling scream from me she sometimes came over to the back door to tell me to come in and get something to eat.

Each morning, I would be up as soon as the sun came up and climbing over my bedmate—although if I was sleeping with Baba, she was always up before me, sitting in an old wooden chair in the backyard. I would run out to tell her that I was hungry, and ask her when we were going to the beach, and she always said "soon," and would get up and meet me in the kitchen, opening the icebox to get out some eggs. Once I had had some breakfast, and changed into my bathing suit, and put my "beach cover-up" (two towels that were sewn together at the shoulders and up the sides, leaving an opening for my head and arms) over my head, I was ready to go!

It took a bit more time for Baba to coordinate with whoever was there that weekend who was taking the car, what groceries or beer needed to be purchased, and by who, and who was arriving that day, so we knew how much supper to make.

Supper was always cold. I don't know if there was a stove in that kitchen, and I am nearly positive there wasn't a BBQ outside. We usually didn't have lunch, but we ate an early supper after we got back from the beach. We had coleslaw, or potato salad made with lots of whipping cream, and garlic sausage, and cold ham, and cucumber salad slathered in sour cream, with lots and lots of fresh dill, and for dessert, maybe some berries someone had picked up at a stand at the side of the road… and sometimes corn on the cob with lots of butter… I think Baba used to boil water in big pot on a little campfire.

Every morning once I was dressed for the beach, Baba and I would walk down the road, past the pump at the end of the street where we got water, and past the public washrooms and showers down a bit of a hill where the paved road stopped and a gravel path started.

In the distance, I would see a huge grassy area, with big willow trees and a raised wooden boardwalk that led past a big A-frame building. The door to the store was always wide open, and there were racks and racks of inflatable balls, inner tubes, towels, sunglasses, flip-flops, beach hats, and a couple of ice cream freezers filled with popsicles and ice cream bars. The minute I saw the store, I started to run down the boardwalk, always hoping that I could run in and have a look around before Baba caught up with me.

Baba loved to look around the store too. She looked at everything and never rushed me out... we just wandered around looking at everything, and once in a while I would put on some sunglasses or grab a fancy beach ball and find Baba to show her, but as we never took any money to the beach, there was never any whining about me wanting Baba to buy me something. (The beach and the cottage was like a million dollar present! What kid in the world could want anything else?)

After we were finished poking around in the store, we would emerge from the front door into brilliant sunshine and that big, blue Manitoba sky, and we would continue to walk down the boardwalk until I could see the sand dunes and I knew the beach on Lake Winnipeg was on the other side.

No matter what time we arrived in the morning, there would always be people already set up with beach blankets and towels, all different colors all over the sand as far as the eye could see. I never remember carrying anything but a big blanket and a couple of towels. Baba *loved* the sun!

Baba couldn't swim... I don't think any of the girls could, although I think Grandpa might have been able to paddle and/or float. I sort of knew how to swim, but I was told the same story from everyone in the family: the lake might look calm and harmless, but there were currents, and something really, really bad called a riptide—when the wind started to blow usually late afternoon, when the clouds formed, and we usually had thunder and lightning. In order to *not* to drown I should stay in the shallow water near the shore and *never* wade out past my knees.

I took these warnings seriously, as I was told several grisly stories of drowned kids… and the way they made it sound, a poor kid drowned every single day!

Baba used to put her hand up to her forehead to block the sun and would take a good look around. We would walk a bit, and eventually find a good spot, sometimes next to another Ukrainian family with a Baba. She would chat with the family in Ukrainian while getting nice and warm in the sun. While this was happening, I was running around like a maniac, sometimes running right up to the water, sticking my foot in and screaming, and then running back to Baba to tell her how cold it was. She would just laugh and say that she was coming soon.

When she was ready, Baba would come down to the water and plop herself down in the sand so that the little waves would wash over her, while she sat with her arms behind her, her hands buried in the sand, keeping herself upright in a sitting position. Now that Baba was right in the water, I got a little braver, running in and out of the lake, or down the shore to see other kids, but I never lost sight of Baba. If I got too far down the beach—which I truly thought was endless—I would hear "Caaaathy…" and start running back.

The water, the sand, the happy laughing people, and a beach blanket warmed by the sun to take a nap on made the day perfect!

When I got hungry, or Baba thought we had had enough sun, we would very slowly gather up the blanket, shake off the sand, and head back to the cottage. I used to hold Baba's hand, and she would tell me who was coming tonight. We would talk about what we were having for supper, and I would tell her how I could help her. I could take the peas out of the shells or wash the carrots and take the tops off or take the hairy stuff off of the corn cobs. I had a little chair in the backyard where she would give me everything I needed, and I would get to work. I also had a little stool in the kitchen where I would stand beside the sink, to keep Baba company while she was peeling potatoes or cucumbers.

When we got back to the cottage, there were cars everywhere, as every cottage had a car full of people coming out to the beach after work. I knew everyone's car, and would be excited to see who would be joining us for the night or a few days.

Sadly, at some point we would have to go back to Winnipeg— usually towards the end of my visit, as I always started my visit at the duplex on McPhillips and ended my visit at Grand Beach.

It always felt like a dream. A warm, sandy, cottage-y dream.

At the end of each summer, a week or so before school started, I would climb back onto the plane and head back home to Calgary. I'd be looking forward to seeing my mom and starting school, but I think if someone had given me a choice I would have moved to Winnipeg for a while.

It All Ends

THERE WAS NO trip to Winnipeg to see Baba in 1973, the summer we left Calgary. We had no money for a flight, and Dad had to start his new job as bakery manager, and I had to get ready to start grade five.

That summer, I stopped being a kid and became an adult. Mom was depressed and pretty heavily medicated and as a result could barely function, so grocery shopping, cooking, laundry, and helping Dad clean government offices three nights a week, all while worrying about starting grade five in a new school, was my new reality.

Baba came to visit once. I remember her sitting with Dad in our little kitchen in the apartment above the bakery where we lived. Dad adored Baba, and the feeling was mutual. Mom never really talked about Baba except with her sisters.

Five years after we moved to Yellowknife, Baba died suddenly after what was supposed to have been routine surgery to have her gallbladder removed. I wasn't allowed to attend the funeral, as Mom didn't have the energy to deal with the death of her mother *and* a distraught fourteen-year-old. I stayed home with David and tried to fathom what a Baba-less world would be like.

I felt completely alone. No one was ever going to look at me like Baba did when she took my face in her hands and brushed my bangs off my forehead making more room for her to examine my face. I was her granddaughter. The only daughter of her oldest daughter.

Years later, when my mom was dying and I had to leave her—unsure if she would be alive when I returned in a week—she did the same thing Baba used to do. She took my face in her hands and really looked at me.

She asked me if we were OK. Our relationship had been complicated, and it was ending far too soon. She wanted a one-word answer—I wished that, like Baba, she could have just loved me and then let me go.

My family never had a good thing to say about Calgary. My dad's third bankruptcy was spectacular in the way it destroyed nearly all of us. In 1973 he was 50, with a ten-year old daughter, a depressed, alcoholic wife, and two sons who had never said goodbye. David went to Edmonton, and Richard got a construction job. Richard used to write my mother letters when we lived in Yellowknife, and she would read them and cry and cry and cry.

Dad had owned three bakeries, and employed both his sons, and was charged and arrested for something—I didn't know what—and as a result, he lost everything. His punishment was driving 1087 miles straight north to assume his new job as bakery manager in an old building in downtown Yellowknife, which included furnished living accommodations for the three of us plus my cat.

The trauma of ten-year old me leaving what she thought was a childhood paradise (complete with cowboys each summer!) simply did not compare with that long, dusty, humiliating drive to Yellowknife in the summer of 1973. I didn't understand what had happened, and had no say in the matter.

I hated them all: Dad for going bankrupt, Mom for drinking and being depressed, and the boys for leaving.

Part 2: Yellowknife

The Long, Dusty Drive

WE ARRIVED IN August, after the longest car ride on the bumpiest partial-gravel road that I had ever driven on.

Calgary to Edmonton was easy. About two hours, past Red Deer and Leduc, and on, straight north. After Edmonton there wasn't a lot to see. Not many towns, or rest stops or gas stations, just miles and miles of nothing but a few scraggly trees. The grassland of the prairies was replaced with rolling hills of rock that looked like a turtle's shell, sort of cracked, with moss and weeds growing out of them. The end of the second day of driving we ended up going through a little town called Hay River, and Dad said that we had left Alberta and were now in the Northwest Territories. It should have been getting dark, but the sun was still high in the sky—which I thought was strange, but I was too tired to care.

We arrived at a huge lake, and we bought a ticket to take the car on the ferry. We were all tired, and sick of being in the car, and Dad said that when we got to the other side of the lake—Great Slave Lake—Yellowknife was just a short drive. As we drove the car onto the ferry, we had all the windows open, as it was so warm. It was August, but I had assumed that as soon as we crossed into the Northwest Territories, we would drive into a wall of snow! We drove onto the ferry, one lone, very dirty Cadillac (since yesterday, missing a muffler) among all the big, black, dirty pickup trucks. We got some looks for sure, and Mom and I stayed in the car on the ferry ride across the narrow part of the lake while Dad got out to stretch his legs and chat with the other guys who had done the same thing. (I think Mom and I were the only females on the ferry that night, but nobody seemed to mind.)

Dad loved to talk to people, and despite the fact that he had a white shirt on, and dress pants, he fit right in with any other working guy. I remember asking him one time if he liked to play golf because Richard Symington's family used to play golf down the hill at the Confederation Golf Course. He looked at me like I was crazy. "Golf?" he said. "Golf? Why would I play golf when I have to work? I have to make money, you know, Cathy." As if I didn't know. As if I didn't understand that was why we had spent two days driving away from our home in Calgary, away from Alberta and the lilacs, and my beautiful room, and Stampede. So he could take a job—he said it was the only good job he could get—as the bakery manager at YK Bakery in Yellowknife, after he had recklessly, foolishly, gone bankrupt for the third time at nearly 50 years old. This trip didn't represent a fresh start; this trip was some sort of lesson… and we were all stuck learning it.

Puss-Puss had woken up and had her front paws on the bottom of the car window looking out at the water, and the birds flying by, and the men walking around on the deck. She turned her head to look back at me as I tried to smooth her messy fur, as if to say, *where are we going?*

The road into Yellowknife was a completely different landscape than I was used to. Low hills of the same rock we had seen for the last 500 miles, but the hills started to grow, and they were covered in moss and lichen in several shades of green and yellow—which reminded me of my plane ride from Calgary to Winnipeg, over fields of canola, wheat, and barley, in green and yellow technicolor.

The road was a bit rough, but Dad seemed to be getting a second wind since talking with the guys on the ferry, and he said that Yellowknife was booming, and there was only one bakery in town.

He said that the bakery was right next door to an old hotel called the Gold Range, and across the street from another hotel called the YK Inn. He sounded excited about meeting the guy who hired him tomorrow morning and having a look around the town, and he told us again that the apartment was really big and that the bakery was right downstairs, and if things got going OK he was going to call David and Richard to come up to work. The guys on the ferry said that there was lots of work in Yellowknife for anyone who wanted to make some real money.

I was only half-listening, as the sun was starting to poke over a hill in front of us as we drove past the sign that said airport, and past another little lake. We had to stop at a stop sign, and I realized that it was almost midnight and the sun was shining in my eyes. Mom put down the visor on her side and told Dad that she couldn't believe the sun was in her eyes in the middle of the night. Dad swung the car to the left and finally the road was smoother, and we went down a big hill and up the other side, past a sign that said Prelude Lake and Old Town with an arrow pointing in the other direction. I wondered if Prelude Lake was like Grand Beach.

As we crested another hill, we saw a little town below us with a bunch of low wooden and concrete buildings, the tallest one maybe five stories. I remembered the view of downtown Calgary as we drove over the Centre Street Bridge, with the Husky Tower, and the tall buildings, and the river snaking through, and the green parks, and Nose Hill—and I had to stop myself thinking as I felt a catch in my throat, already missing home as we drove through this strange place that looked completely deserted in the middle of the night with the bright sun shining.

Dad took another left down an alley, and pulled up behind an old two-story building painted a faded green, with an open back door and a closed screen door, put the car in park, and said, "We're here."

I got Puss-Puss back in her cage, put her cage on top of her litter box, and opened the back door. As I stepped out, Mom was slamming her door and giving Dad a look, and he looked at her and laughed. He told us we didn't have to lock the car, and to come on to see the bakery.

Dad swung open the screen door, and as I walked behind Mom, I heard a bunch of birds cawing from the telephone pole wires, and saw the biggest black crows I had ever seen (I learned later they were trickster-ravens) with shining black eyes and jet black shiny wings. One dropped down from the wire to land on the edge of a huge blue garbage dumpster, poked his head under the lid, and grabbed a plastic bag of old bread—when I walked by, I'm sure that bird thought it was funny that I was carrying a fluffy white cat in a cage.

We walked into a dark cool back room filled with shelves full of sacks of flour, and thought the smell was at least familiar. Dad had had a bakery the entire time I had been alive, and he always came home dusted with flour, smelling faintly of yeast and sugar. We walked through the second door, and as the screen door slammed shut, everyone in the bakery turned around to stare at the three of us.

We must have been a sight. Dad in front, big with his shirt partially untucked from the long drive, his last button undone showing the white ribbed undershirt he always wore. Mom next, dressed in slacks, a short sleeved shirt, and a cardigan sweater, clutching her purse and a mottled blue vinyl airplane carry-on bag—which contained her cigarettes, her pills, her nightgown, an envelope of cash, and whatever jewelry she had left Calgary with. And then there was me. In an old pair of shorts and a t-shirt with a ketchup or grease or pie stain, carrying a cream-colored kitty litter pan and a cage with a meowing Puss-Puss inside.

Of the three bakers standing in front of us, one was black. I don't know if I had ever seen a black man in real life prior to that moment, and his skin was a beautiful dark brown color against his bakery whites. He stepped forward and said to my dad, "Are you Sam?" I think Dad was startled, but he put out his hand to shake his and the man said, "I'm Xavier. You are our new manager? Glenn said you wouldn't be here until tomorrow."

Xavier waved to the other two guys, who went back to work—cutting dough and weighing each piece, rolling it into balls on the bench for rolls, opening the proofing door to pull out a full rack of trays of fluffy buns and bread ready to be moved to the enormous oven that spanned the entire wall. Dad said that he had decided to drive straight through, and he wanted to get us settled in the apartment.

Xavier pointed to a staircase, and said that we should go up the stairs, the door at the top was open, and to come back down if he needed anything. Dad pushed Mom towards the staircase, and I followed, and we walked up the pitch black staircase one by one as I hoped I wouldn't drop the cat.

Dad opened the door at the top, and there was light.

Our New Home

THE DOOR LED into a large room, the center of the apartment. To the right was a kitchen, and as I put down the kitty litter tray and the cat cage, I asked Dad to shut the stairway door so I could let her out. He did, and I squeezed the two pieces of metal together hard enough to release the latch, swung the door open, and told her that she could come out now. This was our new place where we were going to live.

Puss-Puss meowed, and the sound echoed in the almost-empty room. The middle of the apartment was open, and there was a washer-dryer, but not much else. Puss-Puss poked her head out of the carrier for a sniff, but she wasn't quite ready to explore.

We all walked into the kitchen, Mom still hanging onto her things, and Dad talking, telling her that this was a nice kitchen and it had everything we needed. He proceeded to open cupboard doors—each cupboard door was painted a different color, all pale shades of yellow and peach and blue—that held plates I'd never seen before, and glasses, and a toaster, and even a loaf of bread. The stove was tiny and old, but looked pretty clean, and there was even a dozen eggs in the fridge and some instant coffee on the counter. (The man that had hired Dad owned the IGA in town, and I didn't know if groceries were a perk of the job, but in Yellowknife, I was soon to find out, free groceries was a huge savings for us.)

The kitchen sink faced the empty interior of the apartment, facing a further wall with two doors—one was my room, and the other would be (Dad hoped) a room for the boys when they joined us. There was a window in the kitchen that didn't open, and faced a wall, that I found out was the hotel next door. The view was a bit prison-like, but the previous owner had hung some light blue nylon curtains that were swagged back on one side. The curtains sort of reminded me of our living room curtains at home, and I looked over at Mom—perhaps to comment on the similarities. She had still not spoken a word, and was slowly opening each mis-matched-painted kitchen cupboard door, taking a look inside, and closing it again. The countertop was Arborite with a shiny metal border, as was the two- seater table and chairs that sat in front of the large window facing the wall.

Dad had walked into the living room, and had remarked how big it was, and that the reclining lounge chair beside the couch was very comfortable—he pushed the lever to demonstrate, letting out a big "Ahhhh…" as the chair reclined.

I walked into the living room, and the first thing I saw was a bright orange freestanding fireplace against a wall that was wallpapered in birchbark—not wallpaper, real birchbark! *It's beautiful,* I thought. In front of the wall stood a medium-sized TV on a metal stand. The carpeting was bright blue shag, and there was also an old three-seater sofa.

The wall facing the street was a bank of windows, and Dad opened a couple of them, stepping around an old chair and an ashtray also on a metal stand. We immediately heard people yelling and swearing, and as I walked over to look down at the street with Dad, we could see people going in and out of the hotel next door. They were clearly drunk, staggering around, and yelling.

I looked at Dad, and he gave me a look, and turned around and yelled "Lola! What are you doing?" I stood at the window for a while, trying to get my bearings—with the sun, and the lateness, and the new place, for a minute I felt really scared, like maybe this wasn't a good place after all... and maybe we couldn't go back to Calgary.

Dad yelled again, this time for me, and I walked out into the center room, and he walked over to one of the doors and said that this would be my room.

Dad told me I would like my bedroom, and that was an understatement. I had started to cry a little bit at that point, and as I walked through the door, I was shocked at how nice this room was, compared to the other parts of the apartment I had seen already.

The floor was the same linoleum tile, and the room was about half the size of my room in Calgary, but it was clean, and the bed was made, and the furniture was like something out of a fairy tale. Clean and white, with little pink and green flowers in curlicue patterns painted on the headboard and footboard and above the handles on the dresser.

The bed was a single bed, pushed against the wall, but it was a canopy bed, and the canopy and bedspread were thin, fine white fabric, with real embroidery on the canopy ruffle as well as the bed skirt.

There was a window facing the alley that opened, and there was an add-on part to the bakery that meant there was a tar and gravel roof right outside the window. I was relieved because I knew that Puss-Puss would appreciate some outside space. Dad said that he had asked the people who had lived here before to leave all this furniture for me because our Calgary furniture was in storage, and this furniture was much nicer.

I was speechless, either because of the long car ride or the fact that Dad was standing with me in this strange room in this strange town, talking to me about furniture.

I can't imagine what Dad must have been thinking. This was his third bankruptcy, so I guessed the scenario would have been somewhat familiar. Lose everything, gather what you can. Grab the wife and kids and move on to the next town, where no one knows you and start over.

But this time, he was close to 50. This time, his wife wasn't as willing or able to understand why he continued to make the same mistakes, risking everything they (he would have had said "he") had worked for, over and over again. I think this time was also the worst because we had managed to live in one place for ten years, and we had owned that house. And this time, the boys had told him he was on his own—in language I can't repeat—and this time, he had a ten-year-old girl staring at him, unaware that this was how things sometimes went.

He was a dreamer. He was an optimist. Later, when he signed a line of credit for me to open my first business, I realized that. He didn't like working for someone else, and in a strange way, he didn't want that for me either.

Not like the boys, who he convinced to work for him by telling them that they were stupid and wouldn't be able to get a job working for someone else. He had told them that going to school was a waste of time, due to their stupidness, so the sooner as he could get them working for him the better—just like his older brothers had done to him.

I sat down on the bed, suddenly so very tired, and *pssspsssed* for the cat. I told Dad I was going to lie down and read. I would have a look at the rest of the place tomorrow.

As Puss-Puss walked in, gingerly, worried that each step would be quicksand or worse, trying to figure out the smells, with pupils as big as saucers, I pulled back the covers, took off my runners, and crawled into bed.

When I woke up the next morning to the sun streaming through the window, I really had no idea if it was day or night. I looked around, and directly above me, at the very top of the canopy was about a foot of space between two slats and there was a strange, round bulge hanging down.

I got out of bed, and realized I had slept in my clothes, as my suitcase was still in the car. I tried to see what was up there, and all I saw was one paw and a set of ears—and realized that the exhausted cat, like me, had found a place to sleep. When she heard me get up, I heard a faint squeak, but that was about it.

I had to go to the bathroom, and thought I remembered seeing one off the big middle hall, and sure enough the door was open. The bathroom tile reminded me of the tile in Baba and Grampa's duplex... sort of a light pink with black tile edges. There was a toilet and freestanding sink as well as a tub, all the same shade of pink. There was a step up to get in, and the same linoleum tiled floor.

I washed my hands and wondered if anyone else was awake, as I didn't smell any breakfast. I remembered that I had to find the cat food, as I'm sure she was hungry as well.

I walked through the kitchen into the living room and found Mom sitting in the recliner, and saw that someone had brought everything up from the car—probably Dad, who was probably already downstairs working. Mom said good morning, and asked how I'd slept, and I said fine, and she asked me to check in the fridge for something for breakfast. Dad had left a fresh loaf of bread on the counter. She was smoking and drinking her instant coffee.

The frying pan was on the little stove, so I fried some eggs and made some toast, asking if she wanted any. She did not, and as the eggs were frying Puss-Puss came into the kitchen, and I remember thinking that she must have had a tough time getting out of her canopy-hammock—but here she was, meowing for her breakfast! Somebody had put a dish on the floor with some wet cat food in it, beside a bowl of water. I *pssspsst*ed her to come into the kitchen and dragged her over to show her where her breakfast was. She had a few slurps of water and a lick of her food, but she kept looking behind her; she wasn't sure where she was or if she was likely to be attacked by God knows what in this strange place.

I sat down at the little table and ate my eggs and toast, and as I scraped my too-hard egg yolks into the trash, I wondered where

David was. Patty was pregnant, and I thought someone said that they were in Edmonton, as David had gotten a job there.

The breakfast tasted the same as it had in Calgary, but it felt kind of strange to be eating at a kitchen table, staring at a blank wall, instead of on a TV tray in the basement watching TV. After breakfast I asked Mom where Dad was, and what was I supposed to do today and every day until school started in a few weeks. She said that I could unpack my clothes or go downstairs and see if Dad needed some help or go for a walk. Instead, I had a walk around the apartment.

My room looked about the same as it had last night, except I noticed a tall dresser and a low sort of table thing with a small upholstered stool in front of it. I pulled out the stool and had a seat. The fabric was kind of shiny, like satin, and it had the same embroidered flowers that were on the bedspread, curtains, and canopy. There were two deep drawers on the side, and curvy, dainty, spindly legs, which reminded me of horses' legs that I had seen in books.

It took me a while to figure out how to open the top piece. It was the whole top of what I thought was a desk, but pulling the little knobs didn't move anything. When I pulled up on the knobs, however, the entire top opened, and inside was a mirror on the underside of the lid, and below in what I thought was a drawer was a series of divided areas that I suppose could hold a person's jewelry, or makeup, or fancy hairbrushes… of which I had none.

Wait, that is a lie—I did have a handheld mirror and hairbrush of my mother's that sort of reminded me of the stool's upholstery, sort of satiny and shiny. In Calgary, Mom had asked me to brush her hair sometimes, and I always wanted to use the fancy brush that was almost too heavy for me to hold. The mirror had a few brown spots on the glass, as Mom told me that Grampa had given it to her when they lived on the farm in Plumas. Grampa had four girls at home, so when he used to take the horses and wagon into town, he always bought the girls dresses or coats or something pretty like the mirror and brush. Mom said that Grampa knew all the girls' sizes, and would buy all their clothes—even for Baba—and even used to buy them gloves and shoes.

I sat there for quite a while, looking for other secret compartments, opening all the little drawers, and even opening and closing the lid a few times, amazed at how heavy it was. I was trying to imagine what I would put in each compartment, and started to worry that I hadn't packed enough stuff to fill it up. I thought I should start looking through my suitcase and the boxes in the trunk to see what I had actually brought with me, and I started to get a little sad and upset despite the joy of discovering the beautiful little table I was sitting at.

I closed the lid and continued to look around. There was an empty wall with a picture on it. It was pink, maybe a girl all fuzzy, and a pair of ballet slippers in a thin gold frame.

I went next door to the bedroom beside me. The room was *huge*, probably two times the size of mine, with nothing in it but an old brown wooden dresser and two single beds pushed against opposite walls. It had a big closet, unlike my room that had none, and the hanging rail was so high I didn't think I would be able to reach to hang up my clothes. There was a small window with dark blue curtains that were only slightly open, and it reminded me of a room where you would keep someone hidden away. I was even more grateful for my pretty room next door.

Past the bathroom was a hallway with another huge room, with no door on it. It was filled with furniture, and a couple of big rugs, and a lamp, and I couldn't tell if it was our furniture or furniture that had been left in the apartment. The head of the bed, kind of like a bookcase, reminded me of Mom and Dad's bedroom furniture at home, but I think I was still kind of tired, so I couldn't be sure.

At the end of the hall was another bedroom, facing the street, right next to the living room, and it must have been Mom and Dad's room. The bed was made, and there was a dresser and a closet, and in the corner on a small table was Mom's blue vinyl suitcase, with the top open and her clothes still inside.

We lived in Yellowknife in that apartment for nearly two and a half years, and Mom's suitcase remained packed the entire time. Whenever she or I did laundry, her clothes were folded and put back in that suitcase… for the entire time. I remember asking her why she didn't unpack her suitcase, and all she said was "Because we aren't staying here for long."

Getting My Bearings

THE BAKERY WAS down a long, dark staircase, and in order to get outside I had to go through the bakery. There was no light in that staircase unless the top door or the bottom door was open. The bottom door was usually closed, as the flour dust traveled like a cloud, but regardless which door was open I always held my breath going up or down those stairs.

Around the corner from the staircase was a cellar with three or four wooden steps going down. The cellar was filled with bags of flour, and they were piled up as high as they could go, but the ceiling was so low I couldn't even stand up in there, and the floor seemed to be made of rock, not cement. If I pushed aside the flour dust that seeped out of each bag, the floor looked exactly like the rock that I had seen on the drive into town: sort of rounded, and cracked like a turtle shell.

Towards the back of the cellar, it looked like someone had tried to use a jackhammer to dig down a little deeper, but it looked like they had given up after a foot or two. Across from the cellar was the opening to the garage, where the bakery van was parked. The van was old and beat up, rusty in places, and I could see that at one time it had been blue. There was a faint bit of painting on the back windows that read *YK Bakery* in what had once been gold paint.

I walked out of the garage into the alley and saw our Cadillac sitting there looking dirty and out of place, parked beside a couple of old pickup trucks and a small car. I saw the entrance to the back room where we had come in the—night?—before. I was still kind of confused, as I had no idea what day it was or time it was, and it was hard to believe we had already been here a day.

I turned around in the alley to see two or three big dumpsters filled to overflowing with garbage from the bakery, and a couple of guys trying to get the lid open enough to drag out a couple of loaves of bread or buns, squinting into the sun. Across from the alley was a white fence, and a patch of grass, and another street with a low, long building. When I walked over and hopped up on the fence, it turned out to be a Hudson's Bay store. Besides the guys going through the dumpsters I didn't see another person on the street and wondered if it was Sunday.

I got off the fence and turned my attention to the back of the bakery, and noticed that there was a big oil tank with a small ladder to the side of the back door. As far as I could see, if I climbed up the ladder and swung my leg over the oil tank, I would be on the roof that I could see out my bedroom window.

I started to climb, and found it pretty easy to get up onto the roof. The floor was plywood in some places and tar paper in others, and I tried to walk on the raised wooden boards over to my bedroom window. I looked in and could see my unmade bed, and as the door was open, the washer and dryer sitting in the big center hall, and when I crouched down and looked up I could see Puss-Puss fast asleep in the hammock at the top of my canopy bed.

From the roof, I could see the four-story building right beside the bakery—the white stucco wall we looked at through the kitchen window, and on the other side, the remains of a foundation sticking out of the ground, made from white cinderblock and an empty lot beside it. Lastly, a redbrick building on the corner that looked the most like a Calgary building, with a Canadian Imperial Bank of Commerce sign on the side. There were a couple of wooden pallets and an old wooden picnic table on the roof, and not much else, so I thought I would continue my tour of the bakery.

It was a little trickier climbing down, as I had to swing my leg down the outside of the barrel, sliding a bit until my foot hit the first step, and as I was wearing a pair of red and white polka dot fabric clogs with white plastic soles, I lost my shoe on my first try—so I changed tactics. I held onto the metal spout at the top where they must have filled the barrel with oil, flattened myself against the barrel and slid down with both feet until my foot with the shoe still on hit the first step, and as the ladder rungs were metal, I kind of hopped down the other three rungs with my shoed foot, and managed to put my other shoe on, realizing that I didn't have any socks on underneath. I was now smeared with dirt and a bit of oil, all the way down the front of my t-shirt, and smelled a little bit of what must have been oil, but carried on through the back door into the bakery.

Dad was standing at one of the benches, dressed as he always was on a work day. White ribbed undershirt, white shirt, dark gray pants, black belt and shoes. As it was pretty warm, he had rolled up his shirt sleeves, and he was talking with a taller, thinner man. The bakery was empty—so for sure it was Sunday—and I had a good look around.

The bakery looked much the same as our bakery had looked in Forest Lawn, in southeast Calgary. The floor in this bakery was made of wood, not linoleum tile, but it was dusted with white flour, and I saw two big brooms for sweeping propped against the wall. There was a long bench across the front windowless wall, and a large deep fryer especially for donuts. To the right were two big mixers sitting on the floor, cleaned and shining. There were three or four big metal racks, about six feet tall that held big metal trays of buns or cakes, or tarts, or pies... whatever they were baking that day. To the left were the big ovens, a proofing room, and a door to a back room that had a donut filling machine on a table and shorter tables for cake decorating.

Around the corner from the fryer, in the main part of the bakery, was a door with a big piece of glass and a picture window looking out onto the street that had the same gold writing as on the bakery van—although this writing was much brighter and newer. I could read it backwards: *YK Bakery*. This small room was the retail part of the bakery, with a counter that had a cash register and a bread slicer, as well as piles of flat boxes that needed to be put together and could hold a dozen donuts or a cake.

When Dad used to take me to Forest Lawn on Sundays I used to put boxes together or count the float in the till—$50, mostly in pennies, nickels, dimes and quarters, the rest in ones, twos, and fives. This till was empty, as I guess Dad wanted to put the money in on Monday morning... or maybe he was waiting for me to come downstairs and count it?

I bumped into one of the racks with a clang, and Dad and the tall man turned around to stare at me. I'm sure I was a mess, smeared with oil and dirt, my hair uncombed, my face unwashed. Dad told the man I was his daughter Cathy, and I said hi, and he said that he was glad to meet me and asked me if I was excited to be living in Yellowknife. I nodded, and Dad said that I should go back upstairs and finish getting my room organized, as we were going to go out for lunch after he was finished. I said OK, and walked back towards the staircase and out the back door.

I walked to the end of the alley, past the two empty lots, towards the bank, and noticed how dusty the alley was and how there was no grass, flowers, or trees anywhere. The alley ended on a street that had all sorts of big concrete pastel-colored "furniture" or planters and was closed to cars. There were a couple of people around David and Richard's age sitting around in the sunshine talking and laughing—it was good to see people.

The street was long and flat, and there were a few stores. I saw a Marshall Wells, and around the corner the Hudson's Bay, and straight ahead down the street in the opposite direction a store called "The Tog Shop." The window was full of clothes, shoes, purses, and mannequins, and it definitely looked like a "Calgary" store. It was closed, as were the other stores—another sign it was Sunday—so I kept walking past the bank, and when the road became a road again I walked down the sidewalk and saw a library, which was also closed.

Across from the library was a food store, and beyond that, the road sloped down and far into the distance. I could see a bunch of multicolored little houses, and a bit of water, and a few trees. I was starting to get tired and noticed how strong the oil smell was getting as the sun warmed my t-shirt, so I walked back towards the bakery, turned at the CIBC corner, cut through the vacant lot, and saw Dad and the tall man outside the back door smoking. When I got closer they stepped aside so I could pass, and this time I opened the staircase door nice and wide, looked up to see the door closed, took a deep breath and held it, and listened to my echoing footsteps. One, two, three up…

A New Life in a
Few Suitcases

MOM WAS SLEEPING in her room when I got back. I went to my room and found a couple of suitcases and my little carrying case: a small, square, light blue hard-sided case that was supposed to be for a woman's toiletries. But Mom had given it to me, and I used to use it to carry my Archie comic digests and anything else I wanted to take on a short car ride to Banff, or a long car ride to Las Vegas, or Disneyland, or Yellowknife. I snapped open the two brassy-colored locks and peered inside. I didn't remember if I had packed this case, or if like everything else Mom had packed it for me. The contents were unremarkable. Three Archie comic digests, a couple of pieces of paper with notes or lists or drawings. A few random pens, pencils, and crayons, and Mom's little jewelry case that held some costume jewelry she used to wear in her "dancing-dress" years.

I spent a bit of time putting these treasures in my new desk/ makeup table, and I heard Dad come up the stairs. He walked into the living room and called for Mom, then he walked over to my room and asked where Mom was. I told him that she was sleeping, and he asked me if I was hungry. I said I was, and he said that we would go next door and eat, but he would see if Mom wanted to come.

Dad looked at me, and told me to change into some clean clothes and wash my face because it was dirty. I told him I didn't know where the washcloths or the soap were, and he told me to look in the box in the bathroom.

I heard him walk down the hall and I heard a few words from both of them, and as I was going into the bathroom to try to find what I needed, he said, "Let's go." He was hungry too. I asked if Mom was coming and he said she was too tired, but we would pick up some food down the street and make her something later.

My New Job: Everything

DAD TOLD ME that he was starting work tomorrow, and I needed to do some things, like make Mom some food and get my room organized. As we walked down the stairs his words started to echo, and when we got to the bottom of the stairs he picked up a ring of keys that were hanging on a hook beside the garage door, and locked all the doors. As we emerged into the alley, I turned left because I thought we were going to walk down the alley towards the concrete furniture street, but he said, "No, come this way," and we walked down this super narrow passageway between the bakery and the hotel next door. It was cool and dark, and a fan that was sticking out of the hotel wall was making a loud noise, and I could smell the smoke coming out of what I learned later was the bar at the Gold Range Hotel.

We emerged onto a sidewalk, and almost ran into two people who were staggering out of the bar, laughing and talking loudly. They passed us with an "Oh Hi!" and Dad steered me down the sidewalk to the entrance to the café.

The door swung open, and the bell jingled, and we were standing in a big room with a low Arborite counter shaped like a horseshoe to the right, a big pie display case, and a few tables for two and for four. The place was about half full. Everyone turned to look at us, as is the custom in a small town or because we looked so strange. Dad, a big man in a white shirt and dress pants, with his enormous Ukrainian block-head and his black Brylcreemed hair, and this dirty-looking girl looking like she just rolled out of bed and into a mud puddle covered in oil.

The waitress behind the counter was the first to speak. She said to take a seat anywhere, and Dad walked me into the back room (which I learned later was the dining room), and he sat down on a padded bench seat in a booth and told me to sit down in the chair across from him. The waitress came right over and said hi, and wiped the table with a rag, and asked if we wanted anything to drink. Dad wanted a coffee, and he said I wanted a water, and he pulled the menus out of the little stand on the edge of the table that also held the salt and pepper and sugar. When the waitress came back with our drinks, she told us her name was Mary and asked us if we knew what we wanted to eat.

Mary had a very nice smile. She had grayish hair pulled back in a bun, and a uniform that was sort of a mustard yellow, with a white apron with a big pocket where she kept her order pad. Dad gave her a big smile, and I thought that it had been such a long time since I had seen him smile. Lately, he looked like he had a headache when-ever I looked at him. He would smile at Mom every once in a while, but it wasn't his real smile—and both of them knew it because she very seldom looked at him.

Dad asked Mary what was good, and she said that the roast turkey and the veal cutlets were both very good if we were hungry, and when she said that she looked at me and winked. Dad said that we would have two veal cutlets, and she stopped writing for a minute and asked if Dad wanted to see the kid's menu. Dad looked at me and said, "Hungry?" and I nodded, and he told her to bring us two orders. He asked her what kind of pie was fresh, and if they made it there. She said that the lemon meringue and the blueberry were made this morning, and the cooks made them. Dad said that he was the new bakery manager next door at YK Bakery, and he would make sure that his pies were so much better that they would soon be buying them from him—and again, he smiled. He said to bring two pieces of lemon pie after dinner, and told her his name was Sam.

I think Mary actually blushed, and she said it was nice to meet him, and she would put our order in, and it wouldn't be too long. She looked down at me and winked again and walked away.

Dad said that I would be starting school in a couple of weeks, and that Mom wasn't feeling good so I would have to help look after her. He said that he was going to start work tomorrow, and that he had got another job cleaning offices a couple of nights a week, and that I could come with him and do some of the work. He said that he thought that David and Richard might be coming back soon, and when they did, they could have the bedroom next to mine—they were both divorced now, and Patty had taken their baby girl back to Calgary. After the boys made some money, they could get their own place, but before they got here I needed to help look after Mom.

I'm not sure if I understood even half of what he was saying. I remember feeling so tired, and wondering when Mom would get better, and how I was going to go to school *and* go to work with him at night *and* look after Mom, but I nodded like I knew what he was saying.

Mary walked over with our veal cutlets. They smelled so good, smothered in gravy, with two perfect scoops of mashed potatoes and a pile of that perfect frozen vegetable mix of carrots, corn, and peas with a big pat of butter melting on top. (I couldn't remember the last time I had eaten a hot meal at a table.) She also brought us a basket of buns, and Dad said it looked good and asked her to bring him some more coffee. I put my napkin on my lap, grabbed my knife and fork, and started to cut up my cutlets (did I mention they were breaded?) and took my time swirling them around in the gravy before I took a bite.

For the next 15 minutes, we didn't speak. Dad only stopped eating long enough to take a slurp of coffee, and when we were finished, I felt almost brand-new. Mary came by to collect our now empty plates and commented on how hungry we must have been, and both of us let her know how good the food had been. Mary beamed at us, and asked if we still had room for pie. Dad said sure, and as I sat there, happy and full and a little bit sleepy, waiting for my pie (that I was hoping was as good as the meal we had just eaten), Dad asked me what we should take home for Mom for dinner.

When Mary came back with the pie—which looked delicious— Dad asked what kind of soup they had today. Mary said it was a vegetable barley, and Dad said that we would take a big bowl to go, and said to put two buns and some butter in the bag as well. Dad and I ate the tangy, lemony, sweet pie, and as I could only eat half of mine he asked Mary to put it the rest in with the soup, as we were taking the soup home for his wife, who was tired from the drive.

Mary asked where we had come from. I said Calgary, and Mary looked at me like I was from Mars. "You drove all the way here from *Calgary?*" she exclaimed, with one hand on her hip. So I proceeded to tell her about Puss-Puss, and the ferry. As Dad had gotten up, I got up too, and I told Mary that I had an aunty named Mary and that my brothers were both in Edmonton but were coming soon, and that I would be starting grade five in a few weeks, and that we lived next door above the bakery in a big apartment. Mary put her arm around me and told me that was wonderful because she would see me all the time, and gave me a squeeze and a smile and a wink.

I started to cry as Dad paid the bill and told me that we had to get back, because Mom was probably hungry, and when I turned around, Mary was waving, so I waved too.

YELLOWKNIFE PEOPLE

DAD STARTED WORK the next day, as promised, and after breakfast I started to put my clothes into my new dresser—but I quickly lost interest and walked into the living room where Mom was sitting in her chair. I said that I was going out to visit the library and get myself a library card. She said OK, and she would see me later, but her voice was flat and she didn't look at me. It was as if it was too painful for her to turn her head. I asked her if she wanted me to turn the TV on, and she said no, so I left.

The bakery was full of people when I got to the bottom of the stairs. A blonde guy was carrying trays of bread from a stack near the cellar and loading them into the bread van. He looked a little older than Richard, but I couldn't be sure. He had long blonde hair—Dad always said a man's hair was long if it touched the top of his shirt collar, but this guy had on a yellow t-shirt, wide legged jeans, and runners, and I couldn't believe Dad let him work there. The boys were *never* allowed to wear jeans at work, but I guess this guy was a delivery guy, so maybe Dad didn't mind.

Dad was standing near the front counter in the corner talking to a tiny little Chinese woman. She was looking up at Dad, and they were looking at some sort of ledger. There were the same three bakers working as the night we had arrived—Mr. Xavier and the other two guys. They were almost in the same positions: Mr. Xavier at the bench rolling buns with both hands and cutting dough with a metal scraper, plopping each dough ball onto the scale. As I walked past, he saw me and said, "Hello again, my dear! I have forgotten your name."

I said my name was Cathy Yurkiw, and he reached out his flour-covered hand to shake-squeeze mine and said it was nice to see me again, and told me that his name was Xavier. He had a beautiful smile, and I noticed how the streak of flour on his cheek looked so bright against his deep brown skin. He had sparkly dark eyes, just like the ravens, and I said that I was pleased to meet him, and he threw his head back and laughed.

Dad turned around when he heard him laughing, and saw me standing there, and told me to come over and meet Lily. Lily wasn't much taller than I was and was slim like a young girl, but you could tell by her face that she was older than that. Dad told her my name, and she said hello. She had a pretty strong accent, but she said my name a couple of times—I think so she could remember it.

Dad said that Lily was going to run the front of the bakery and schedule the guys, and I should check with her if she needed me to do anything. I nodded and said that I was going to go to the library, get a library card, and check out a couple of books because I couldn't find any upstairs. He said OK and asked me what Mom was doing, and I said, "Nothing." He sighed.

Dad said that in a couple of days I was going to go on a tour of Giant Mine with a girl about my age named Marilyn Glick. Her dad owned a clothing store down the street called "The Tog Shop," and we could be friends. I had no idea what Giant Mine or a tour of it was, but I said OK and walked out the front door just as a customer was walking in. I still had no idea what time it was. It was the strangest feeling, not knowing if it was 7 a.m. or 11 p.m.

In Calgary, we had a clock on the wall in the kitchen above the sink. Dad and Mom both wore watches. Mom's was so tiny. It had been a gift from Grampa and had three tiny little stones above and below the face. The glass was rounded over the numbers, and the glass had gotten a little dirty over the years, and I could never figure out what time it was.

Despite the fact that I was starting grade five, I would have problems telling time for the entire time I lived in Yellowknife. I was unsure if the problem stemmed from having to tell time in French before I truly understood how to tell time in English, or the fact that Yellowknife really only had two seasons: daylight all the time and then darkness all the time.

I thought that time wasn't really important to me. I didn't really have to be anywhere at any time until school started in a few weeks, and before then, perhaps someone would find our Calgary clock and put it up in the kitchen. All I knew was that it was Monday, and the sun was up, and everyone was busy.

I had slept through the bright, sunny night, only opening my eyes once or twice while rolling over to notice that the sun was sort of going down and the sky had gone from blue to a light purple that reminded me of the lilacs in Calgary, but before I could start thinking about that I had fallen back asleep. My single bed was against the wall, and if I rolled over too far, I banged my head or my nose on the wall and had to re-adjust myself with a sigh.

My window had stayed open all night, as I liked to hear the ravens in the back alley having their conversations—alternatively cawing and clicking their raven tongues, sometimes landing on the roof, sometimes swooping by and dropping a treasure for me to find the next day.

The ravens were *huge* in Yellowknife. I had never seen birds that big. You could hear them flying past and feel the air move above you when they flapped their beautiful black wings.

In Calgary you always saw healthy birds and birds that looked a little sickly. In Yellowknife, despite the fact that all the ravens in the back alley seemed to feed on stale bits of bread and the occasional bit of food thrown out by the café next door at the hotel, they were the healthiest, smoothest, shiniest-feathered creatures, with eyes like black marbles, but bigger.

I was never scared of them. I used to talk to them, as they were always squawking and clicking, and I swear I heard them speak a word or two on several occasions. Once, I swear they were taking turns imitating Puss-Pusses' meows.

When I walked around town, it was kind of comforting to look up and see a raven that looked like a raven in the alley following me. They flew from telephone pole to telephone pole, to tops of buildings, to tops of scrawny trees, their weight nearly bending the poor tree in half.

THE LIBRARY

THE FRONT SIDEWALK was shaded, and as I walked up the street towards the bank, I decided to go straight through when the light turned green, and then realized that there were a few cars and trucks on the road. There were a few more shops and across the street was the IGA food store. Dad had said that the man who had hired him as the bakery manager owned the IGA and the bakery.

The store looked new. It was bright white stucco, with a nice sign that said IGA, and people were going in and out. I crossed at that corner, and wondered if that was where we were going to drive to get groceries.

I continued back to the corner where The Tog Shop was, and turned down the street towards the library.

I loved to read; Mom said I could read by the time I was three, and that I preferred to read on my own than to have someone read to me. The library seemed a little farther than I remembered, but today there were people on the street and cars driving by, so the walk was more exciting than it had been on Sunday.

I had to cross the street again when I saw the library, and checked the hours on the door, and when I saw someone come out, I realized it was open, and walked over to the front desk.

I told the woman behind the counter that my name was Cathy and I had just moved to Yellowknife from Calgary, and I wanted to get a library card to be able to check out some books. She said that I needed to fill out a form, which she gave me, as well as a pencil—I asked if I could fill it out right there, or if I'd have to move. She said to go ahead and stay where I was, and I started to fill in the form.

I did my name, but when I got to my address, I had no idea. I asked her if I should put my Calgary address because we were living in an apartment above the YK Bakery, and I didn't know the address. She looked at me and smiled. I thought that she looked like a librarian. She had glasses and light brown hair that was piled in a bun on top of her head, and a nice top with and orange and red flower print and a cardigan that matched the orange. She said that we could find my address in the phone book, and she pulled out a slim book and looked up YK Bakery in the Yellow pages, and asked if I wanted to write the address. I said yes, please, and she told me that I lived at 5015 50th Street. I wrote down the address, and then she asked my phone number, which I began to explain that I didn't know, but I had memorized my Calgary phone number. She said that was fine; I should write down the phone number for the bakery, which I did.

I received my library card, and I asked her what section I should look in for a couple of books to read. She asked me how old I was, and she took me over to the kid's section—I must have made a face, so she took me over to the "young adult" section, which looked much more interesting. I told her that I had already read a few Nancy Drews, and asked what she would suggest. She said, that as I was new to Yellowknife and to the North, she would suggest I start with *Lost in the Barrens* by Farley Mowat. The story was about a young man who went on an adventure up north, but she said that parts of it could be a little scary.

She handed the book to me, and I asked how many books I could take out at one time and she said three or four. The whole time, she was looking at me with a puzzled look on her face, and she asked if

I had a bag to carry the books and wanted to know where my mom and dad were. I told her that my mom had depression and my dad was working today, and she said that was fine, just to bring as many books as I wanted to check out up to the counter—and she would tell me what was happening at the library because I might want to join in.

I checked out *Lost in the Barrens* and *Anne of Green Gables*, and she said that I had made two good choices. She said she would see me in a couple of weeks when I had finished reading them, and gave me a flyer that listed all the activities that were happening at the library. She told me that I was welcome to stay at the library and read, and I almost did, as this library reminded me of the library down the hill from our house near Northmount Drive that Mom used to take me to—but I was starting to feel a bit hungry, so I took my two books and headed back to the bakery. Stupidly, I forgot to ask the librarian the time…

Marilyn and Giant Mine

A FEW DAYS later, Dad said that today was the day that I was going to meet Marilyn and we were going to tour Giant Mine.

Marilyn had just arrived in Yellowknife as well. She walked down to the bakery with her dad and my dad drove us out to the mine. It was the first time I had been in the car since we had arrived, and Marilyn and I sat in the back while Dad drove. I showed her all the fancy car things in the back seat, like the footrests and the trays and the reading lights, and as we pulled out of town and went down the big hill towards Prelude Lake the landscape became more and more empty.

I asked Marilyn if she had ever been to a mine before, and she shook her head. She was a little taller than me, but we both had brown hair and eyes. She had much nicer clothes than me, but her dad did own a store. I asked where she had come from and she said a place called Toronto, a long way away. She said that they lived in a house. She couldn't believe we lived above the bakery.

After a little while on the road I saw a really tall crane-looking thing, and Dad said that we had arrived at the mine. When he stopped the car, he said the miners were looking for gold, and if I found any I should bring some home! He walked Marilyn and

I over to a man with a hard hat, near an office and told him our names, and the man asked another man to get us some hard hats too, and we would get going.

Our hats were pretty big on us, but he showed us how to pull the straps under our chin tight, and he said to follow him. We waved goodbye to Dad, and when I looked back, he was talking to one of the guys, and they were both smoking. I heard the guy ask if Dad wanted to go with us, and he said, "No way he was going down there," and they both laughed. I wondered where "down there" was…

The man was telling us about the mine, but I couldn't hear very well, as my hard hat came down over my ears, but we both nodded a lot. He told us that it was going to be a little cold and dark in the mine, but that we might find some gold! He walked us over to a sort of metal box thing that was open on the sides, but not on the top and bottom, and we stepped inside. He asked if we were ready, and he said that we were going down shaft number one. He grabbed a small metal box with a big red button on it, said, "Here we go," and pressed the button, and with a big lurch we were going down into the earth.

I was too scared to scream. It was the worst ride I had ever been on, and I closed my eyes and tried to pretend I was on a ride at the Stampede. Marilyn grabbed my hand, and we just hung on to each other as the elevator went down and down and down. I remember the smell of earth and metal, sort of like tin cans, and when we slowed down after what seemed like an hour, I opened my eyes, and it was pitch dark.

The man swung the door open, and straight ahead was a long tunnel with lights hanging from the roof of this enormous cave made out of rock and dirt. We must have looked terrified because the man stepped out of the elevator and asked if we were OK. We nodded, and he said we should follow him.

I wasn't sure if I could move or walk, but I knew I wanted to get out of that metal cage. I took a couple of steps—still hanging onto Marilyn—and a couple of gulps of air. I realized I must have been holding my breath all the way down, like I did on the stairs in the bakery. The air smelled and tasted like dirt and water, and it was so incredibly dark, and there was this strange feeling of pressure that didn't match the height of the cave. I felt like I was being pushed down.

After a few breaths of air and a glance at Marilyn—whose eyes were so wide they looked like a cat's eyes when they are really scared or ready to pounce—the man leaned down to look at us and asked us again if we were OK. I blurted out that I wanted to go back up, and Marilyn didn't speak, and the man said that he just wanted to show us where the gold was, and then we would go upstairs to look at some pictures. He asked us if that was OK.

I think because I had started to breathe again, I said OK, and Marilyn nodded. The man started talking about when they found gold in Yellowknife, and how long the mine had been operating, and how many tons of gold they had taken out over the years, and we started walking down the tunnel.

We could hear a bit of noise further down and see some lights, and we walked for a while. The man stopped when we were quite close to a bend in the tunnel, where the noise was getting louder, and he asked us to come closer to the wall. It was a little darker the further away you got from the hanging lights from the top of the cave, but he pulled a small flashlight out of his pocket and shone it at the cave wall a little above our heads. The wall changed from black to an iridescent color to gold as he moved the flashlight beam around. The gold color was the brightest, and it looked like a jagged bolt of lightning all the way up the wall, He said that we could touch it, and we did, and then he shined the flashlight on our fingers, and they were covered in gold dust. He said that we were both rich now, and our fingers were covered with at least one hundred dollars worth of gold dust between the two of us. We just stared at him and said, "Wow." He said that we should put our hands in our pockets to save the gold, and we did just that, and he told us that this mine had more gold in it than they could ever take out, and they would still be taking gold out of it for a thousand years.

The man shined the flashlight beam up and down the curved walls of the tunnel, and we saw gold everywhere—even on the dirt floor where we were walking. After we had a look around, he said that it was time to go back up to the surface.

Marilyn and I were both feeling better by then. I think the shock of the ride had worn off, and we hopped into the elevator, and he looked at us and said "Ready?" We nodded, and he hit the magic button, and with a lurch we were headed up, up, up, towards the sun.

Puss-Puss's First Life

ONE DAY THE sky went dark, and we got a heavy thunderstorm... like the ones in Calgary and Winnipeg, but this one started in the morning and lasted all day long. Thunder boomed all day, followed by some spectacular lightning that was so bright, I could see it long after I closed my eyes to the flash. I wasn't sure where Puss-Puss was, but I had been in my room all day reading, as it was also pouring rain. She wasn't in her little hammock, and she wasn't in the big room with the piled up furniture and rugs. My bedroom window was only open a crack, so she wasn't on the roof. I was starting to panic. She very seldom went downstairs to the bakery. If she did sneak out when the top or bottom door was open, she usually slinked around the corner into the cellar looking for a mouse or a rat to chase.

After I had asked Mom if she had seen her anywhere, I went downstairs to check the cellar. She was mostly white, like the flour bags, but was a calico, with big brown and black patches, so she was pretty easy to spot even if she was scared by the storm and was hiding—but she wasn't there. I went into the bakery and asked Lily and Mr. Xavier if they had seen her, and they said no, but they would tell me if they found her.

I walked into the back room, calling her, and looked out the screen door into the raging storm and thought that if she had gone out the garage, I would never find her... and a raven had probably eaten her.

I walked back up the stairs and into my room, and Mom yelled out, "Did you find her?"

I yelled back, "NO!" and walked over to my bedroom window, scanning the alley looking for a wet patch of white, black, and brown. And then I heard it: *Mrowr*. And I cranked open the window and listened again. *Mrrrrooowwwrrr*. And I knew it was her, and she was out in the rain, and I had to find her.

I threw on my hoodie, and as I got to the door Dad was just coming in. He asked if I had found the cat. I said no, but I heard her meowing outside, and I was going to find her. He asked where I heard her, and I said the alley, and I started to run down the stairs, and he followed. We both stood at the back screen door, and I heard another forlorn *Mrowr*—he heard it too, and I said that I thought it was coming from the empty lot next door and wondered if she had fallen into the half-finished basement foundation and couldn't get out or was drowning...

I was yelling this as I sprinted past the potholes in the alley, and as I got closer the meowing got louder. I started screaming her name, and the meowing got louder, and by the time Dad had caught up with me I had seen her, crouched in a corner, soaking wet, looking up at me.

I had no idea how she had gotten down there, and no idea how we were going to get her out. Just then, a huge clap of thunder sounded, and she scurried into a dark corner, out of sight on her narrow concrete ledge.

Dad swore, and ran back to the bakery to get a flashlight. He told me *not* to move, that he would be right back. I kept calling her and telling her we were going to get her out of there, and she kept meowing back, and the meows were so loud now, people on the street hurrying by were slowing down to ask if I needed help. I said that my dad was coming, and one lady came over to stand beside me with her umbrella as I was soaked and shaking.

I kept looking down and thinking that the water at the bottom looked deep, and I had no idea how were going to rescue her. Dad came walking over, carrying a small stepladder and a flashlight, and told me to run upstairs and get her cage, because she was scared and might not let us hold her.

I ran and got the cage, and by the time I got back there were three people with umbrellas helping Dad with the ladder and shining the flashlight in the corners, and Dad was already down in the hole telling her that we were going to take her home if she would stay put and stop running around. I put the cage on the edge of the white cinderblocks, and a big bolt of lightning lit up the sky. Dad hopped off the ladder into the water and made a grab for her. He caught her, dragged her meowing and hissing across the top of the water, and shoved her in the cage, which I snapped closed.

The three people gave a little cheer, and one of the men helped Dad up the ladder. The water was up to his knees, so I could see his shoes were ruined, and both of us were soaking wet. He thanked the people, and the three of us walked slowly back to the bakery—one of us meowing in the most pitiful way, almost hoarse—and I couldn't believe the rescue mission had been a success.

This adventure must have scared her as much as it scared me because for the next two and a half years, she never set one paw outside (except for her regular constitutions on the roof). When I let her out of the cage upstairs, and Mom and I toweled her off, she climbed onto the bed, and cleaned her fur for two hours before falling asleep for the better part of the next 24.

I was convinced that one of her nine lives had been used up… and from that day on, she regularly curled around Dad's legs in the morning in the kitchen, as she knew that he had surely saved her from a watery grave.

FORT RAE

THERE WAS A week to go before school started, and I was driving everyone nuts, as I am impatient, and I wanted to start school, meet some other kids, and start learning instead of hanging around in back alleys.

I knew I would be starting school on the Monday after the long weekend. Dad had hung a bakery calendar in the kitchen above a little table that had a black phone on it and had circled the date. A clock had also appeared, so I was getting more used to recognizing the time of day.

Dad said that my school was brand new, and was something called an open-area school, and I could walk there. He said that he would take me to Marshall Wells for a new pair of jeans, and said he would show me how to use the washing machine so I had some clean t-shirts for school. I wanted to know why we weren't going back-to-school-shopping at The Tog Shop. Dad said it was too expensive, and that I had lots of clothes. He said he would take me to the Bay in a month or so because I would need a parka for the winter and a pair of boots.

I was excited to start school as I was bored and tired of being alone every day. I had been helping Dad clean the government offices, helping Lily downstairs in the bakery make boxes, and even slicing some bread. I had been walking to the grocery store to pick up food anytime Dad gave me a handful of money and a list, and I had been reading my library books.

I moped downstairs one day, had a look at the calendar on the wall, and realized there was *still* one week plus a long weekend before I started grade five in my new school. I hadn't seen Marilyn since that day in the mine; every time I stopped by her dad's store, he said that she was out with her mom or on a trip or something. As I asked Dad for the 100th time what should I do today, he said that I was going to drive with the blonde guy—Ryan, the bread van driver—to Fort Rae to deliver some bread. The drive was little over an hour, and I could see another town and keep Ryan company.

I thought this was a great plan, and it would kill most of the morning. He told me to find Ryan and help him finish loading the van. I walked through the garage, and I couldn't believe how much we were taking to Fort Rae! There must have been 15 trays of bread stacked up right to the top of the van, and trays of donuts, and pies, and even a couple of birthday cakes. Ryan came out of the bakery with a few big bins filled with bags of buns, and a couple of boxes of butter tarts and squares. He dropped them on the garage floor, and climbed in, wiggled himself to the front, and asked me to pass them to him. I went back into the bakery a couple of times to bring what was left in the pile marked Fort Rae, wondered how big the town was, and wondered why people just didn't drive to Yellowknife to pick up their bread and anything else they wanted.

When the van was full, Ryan wiggled to the front seat, and out the driver's door, and scared me when he came up beside me and slammed one of the back van doors shut—then laughed when I jumped, and slammed the other one. He was tall and super thin with long, blonde, wavy hair, and his hair was so blonde I barely noticed he had a mustache. He said that I should use the bathroom if I needed to, and he was going to grab a coffee. He asked me if I wanted one, and when I looked surprised, he laughed again and said we were leaving in a few minutes, 'cause we had to fill up with gas and get going.

I went upstairs to pee, yelled "Bye," to Mom, who asked where I was going and I said Fort Rae. And when she asked where that was, I was already halfway down the stairs, so I yelled back, "Ask Dad!" and I hopped into the passenger seat of the van.

Ryan showed up a few minutes later with Dad, and Dad told me to put on my seatbelt and said that I could meet him in the café for lunch when I got back. Ryan made some crack about how come he wasn't getting lunch, and Dad told him not to be a smart-ass and not to drive like a maniac. Ryan started the van, and we were off.

We drove down the pothole-filled, dusty alley, and drove towards the one gas station I remember seeing. Everything in Yellowknife was expensive, but gas was about ten times as expensive as it had been in Calgary, and the van was really heavy—I hoped we wouldn't run out. Ryan filled the tank, plus a medium-sized orange gas tank bungee corded to the back bumper of the van, so I guess he was worried too. He paid for the gas and came back with a pack of cigarettes and a KitKat bar, and tossed the KitKat onto my lap. It was already warm, and I thought I had better eat it before the chocolate started to melt.

We left town in a direction I had never gone before, and I saw a bunch of houses and a couple of trailer parks, and then we were on an empty road—which was paved at first, but in a few miles turned into gravel. The van wasn't air conditioned, so we had the windows wide open and the radio cranked up, but when we hit the gravel road, we had to roll up the windows almost to the top because of the dust, and we kept losing the radio. We listened to CBC, some strange people calling in to talk about something, and once in a while an old song I didn't recognize—and then static for a couple of miles. There were no more houses, and a few small trees were about all there was to look at. Once, a red pickup truck came screaming up behind us, and passed us, and sprayed gravel all over the van, and some of the rocks hit the windshield that was already full of cracks. Ryan said that the guy was an asshole, and he would have to tell Dad that the damage wasn't his fault. He asked what grade I was going into and what Calgary was like.

Ryan was from "way back East" in New Brunswick, a place I had never heard of, and he said that he had hitchhiked all the way to Yellowknife. It had taken him a couple of weeks, and he liked it, but he might go back home before the winter. I told him all about Calgary: The Stampede, Nose Hill, my brothers, and Mom's depression, and he looked at me kind of sad a couple of times. He said that he was sure that things would work out, and because I was from Calgary the winter would be no problem for me (except for the darkness).

The darkness was very weird, he said. He had lived in Yellowknife for three years, and he still wasn't used to the complete darkness that happened around Christmas. He said that Caribou Carnival was just like Stampede, with dog sled races instead of the rodeo, but I would love it. He said by the time the end of March rolled around everybody was ready to party, and that the Carnival took place on the lake on top of about 12 feet of ice. I must have looked worried, so he said that much ice would never break, and he said people drilled holes in the ice all the time to go fishing!

I spotted a road sign that said Fort Rae, but I didn't see a fort—or much of anything. We kept driving, and turned onto another road, and Ryan said that the people in Fort Rae were always happy to see the bakery van arrive. I could see some low buildings ahead of us, and a small crowd of people. He slowed down, and I saw people running towards us on the road and beside the road. Mostly kids, but some adults, and some adults holding kids.

Ryan slowed down some more, and he told me to roll down my window and he did the same, and by the time everyone caught up to us, they were all laughing and saying hi, and running and bouncing up and down. It was like we were famous!

We pulled up to a building that looked like a corner store right beside the Hudson's Bay—but it didn't look like the Bay in Yellowknife. It was quite small, and the writing in gold on the window looked kind of old-fashioned, and there were fur pelts hanging in the window.

Ryan stopped and turned off the van, and said that I could stay in the van or get out and stretch my legs, but him and the guy who owned the store would do the unloading.

I opened my door, and there were a whole bunch of people crowded around the van. Some of them patted me on my shoulder and said hi, and some of them wanted to take my hand. They were beautiful brown-skinned people with beautiful smiles, and dark eyes like mine that crinkled up almost to nothing when they smiled… and in the half an hour or so that we stayed in Fort Rae, they never stopped smiling or laughing!

Some of them said hi, and I said hi back, but they mostly wanted to dance around the van, looking in the back and following Ryan and the other guy into the store with the bread trays. The little kids and the babies were so cute! Some of them were on their mom's backs, and some of them were walking a little with another older kid holding their hands to make sure they didn't fall. Most of the kids didn't have shoes on, but some of the adults had on sort of slipper shoes made out of a goldy-tan material, with beads in the shape of flowers on the front, and sometimes bits of fur at their ankles. Besides "hi," I didn't hear any English words, so I must have said hi a million times.

By the time Ryan and the guy from the store had re-loaded the van with the empty trays, most of the people were milling around the front of the store, and when people came out with a loaf of bread or a bag of buns, everyone would kind of give a little cheer, and they would look at what they had.

Ryan got in and started the van and asked if I was ready to go. I said sure, and hopped up into the seat and put my seatbelt on.

I only visited Fort Rae once, but I can still see everyone waving at us through the small back windows of the van as we turned the corner and got back onto the road to Yellowknife.

GRADE FIVE... AT LAST

Finally, THE SEPTEMBER long weekend came and went, and I started grade five. The school was a new concept—open-area—and much different than the traditional redbrick, one-level elementary school I had done grades one to four in. I was wearing my new jeans, and a clean pair of runners, and a t-shirt with a cardigan sweater. I said goodbye to Mom upstairs, and to Dad and Mr. Xavier and Lily downstairs, and walked out the back door across the alley to the small white fence and climbed over it.

I walked past the Bay and around the corner, and crossed the street at the old brick high school—and at that point I saw lots of kids being dropped off, or walking together down the streets from every direction. It was the busiest I had ever seen the streets since I arrived a few weeks ago.

The school was sort of a round shape, set back from the road, with a playing field and parking lot in the front. It was about half a block from the high school, which looked much like the tan sand-stone schools that were built all over Calgary except that it was clad half in in wood, half in brick. My school was softer-looking, clad in a material that could have been wood, but might have included some concrete and perhaps some metal.

I fell in line with a bunch of kids who were getting dropped off on the sidewalk by their parents, and some of them were laughing or smiling, and some of the ones that looked a little nervous were getting hugs from their parents. I caught a couple of kids' eyes, and wondered if they knew I was not from here, and wondered the same thing about them.

The sidewalk was long, and when it got to the school, it kind of wrapped around the front, and I began to see what I assumed were teachers who were holding the doors open and saying hi to all the kids, directing them into the gymnasium for a sort of first day assembly. The school smelled brand new, and it was very clean and shiny inside, to match the outside.

I followed a bunch of kids into the gymnasium, and we all sat in the bleachers and waited for something to happen. After all the kids filed in, the gymnasium wasn't even half full, so they asked us to move to the middle, closer together.

I noticed that some of the kids had backpacks and gym bags, and some of them were getting papers and pencils out, but I didn't have anything, so I made a mental note to pay attention so, at least, I knew which homeroom I was supposed to go to.

Soon the microphone was turned on, and we were all asked to stand up and sing "O Canada," and I saw a flag and a picture of the Queen way up above the basketball hoop. We finished the song and sat down and listened to the principal talk about how glad he was to have us here in this new school. He told us that we should pay attention to our teachers, who would tell us where our classrooms were, and that the difference in this school was that we needed to walk back and forth to classrooms very quietly so we wouldn't disturb the other students—because the classrooms only had one wall and no doors!

I was trying to figure out what a one-walled classroom would look like, and then the assembly was over, and we were asked to form lines in front of the desk in the middle of the floor with our grade on it, and they would take attendance and walk us to our classroom (very quietly).

I was relieved that they had my name on the list, as I don't remember anything about Mom going to register me for school, and I was starting to get excited to see the rest of the school. Before long, we were reminded to stay quiet, and follow our teacher, and we were off. Once we were up the stairs, I could see the classrooms, each with one wall that had a big chalkboard with the teacher's desk in front of it, and then rows of desks.

My classroom was at the top of the staircase to the left and the library was right in the middle of that floor, fully accessible to all the classrooms. The room that I would learn French in had a wall of glass, and maybe two walls in total, because learning French required a lot of repetition and we would be a little noisier than a regular classroom. We were shushed quite a bit on the walk—not in a mean way, but in a way to remind us that there was no talking in between classrooms. Compared to the noise in my elementary school, I found it quite nice. The beautiful surroundings and the quietness made me feel kind of safe, and relaxed, and less stressed than I had been since we arrived, and I knew from that first day that I was going to love this school.

Grocery shopping was one of my jobs when we moved to Yellowknife, and before I started shopping, I liked to stand at the community board and stare at all the announcements, and read about the stuff people had for sale and the things that people needed, like a roommate or a babysitter. The first time I went shopping after school started, I saw a poster saying that girls aged 9 to 12 were welcome to register for Brownies. I was so excited to meet some other girls my age, and they mentioned going to meetings, and earning badges and going camping; I was instantly ready to be a Brownie! I asked one of the cashiers to write down the phone number and the date and time and place for registering, and I would let Mom know that I wanted to be a Brownie.

I practically skipped around the grocery store with all the information in my jeans pocket. I got my groceries and stopped by the library to ask if there were any books on Brownies, and when there weren't, headed home. When I got upstairs I dropped the groceries on the counter, and told Mom—who was sitting exactly where she had been sitting when I left for school in the morning, in the reclining chair near the door from the living room to the kitchen—about Brownies. She said that I should ask Dad and told me to leave the piece of paper by the telephone on the little desk.

When Dad came upstairs a few hours later I told him all about it, and he didn't seem too thrilled about me going to meetings somewhere at night by myself, but said if I wanted to it would be OK if Mom said it was OK. Mom said that I would need a uniform, and she would need to find out where the meetings were, but she would call tomorrow when I was at school, and we could talk about it after school tomorrow.

I went to bed that night dreaming about my new uniform and all the badges I would try to earn, and the meetings and camping. By the second week in September, the days were getting shorter, and by the time I went to bed it was actually a little dark and getting cooler. Puss-Puss liked the cooler weather, and slipping out of the bedroom window at night when I was doing my homework (so she could avoid the majority of day-ravens, as they seemed to all fly off to somewhere else at night), and she could enjoy some safety on the exposed roof after dark. Her white fur glowed like a little moon, and when she jumped back through the window before I went to bed, she felt fluffy and cold, almost frosty, and I wondered how long it would be before the snow would start to fly.

OUTSTRETCHED HANDS

ONCE I WAS in school, about a month after we arrived, Dad told Mom that Glenn and his wife (Glenn was the man who owned the IGA and the bakery) and Mary and Milo had both invited the three of us over to their place for dinner. Mom wasn't keen on the idea, but Dad said that we should go because Glenn was his boss. We told Mom that Mary was really nice because Dad and I had had lunch with her husband Milo a couple of times at the café, and he was a really funny guy.

As I listened to this conversation one night as we ate dinner in the living room, I thought what a difference between Yellowknife and Calgary. In Calgary Dad had worked seven days a week, coming home each night to eat and fall asleep on the couch. In Yellowknife, he wanted to be social!

Mom said she had nothing to wear, not even a warm jacket, so Dad said he would go and get her one the next day—and on the next Saturday we went to Glenn's, and the following Saturday, to Mary and Milo's. Dad bought parkas for both of us, and a new blouse for Mom, and we got into the Cadillac—which hadn't been started since Dad had driven Marilyn and I to Giant Mine—and drove a few minutes to Glenn's house.

It was a very nice house. A little smaller than our Calgary house, but it was so nice to see Mom put lipstick on and Chanel No. 5 and the ring Dad had bought her for their 25th wedding anniversary. She smiled and talked with Glenn's wife, and Dad and Glenn drank a beer and talked about business and how we liked Yellowknife so far. They had a daughter who was a few years older than me, and she came out of her room a little while after we got there and showed me around her house, and we talked about where they had come from while we sat in her room. She had an older brother, but unlike mine, he was at University in Toronto—so they wouldn't see him again until Christmas.

Then it was time for dinner. We had roast beef, mashed potatoes, and gravy, and cake for dessert. We sat at their dining room table, and Mom and Glenn's wife had some red wine, and I saw that Mom had some color in her face. She was even laughing a bit at what Glenn was saying, and for a minute I felt like things were normal, and we could have been back in Calgary.

I started to think about my old house, and I didn't want to start crying at this lovely dinner, so I kept eating and drank my diet Pepsi and smiled at everyone at the table.

Glenn must have seen my shining eyes, and said that he would make some coffee, and when he walked past my chair, he gave my shoulder a squeeze.

Our next dinner was at Mary and Milo's. It was starting to turn cold, and the sun was going down every night now. Dad told Mom and me that we were invited for dinner, so we put on our new parkas, got in the Cadillac, and drove about ten minutes to arrive at a smallish house with a mailbox at the end of the sidewalk and what looked like nice curtains hanging in the front window.

The house looked old, like all the houses in Yellowknife, but this one was painted a brighter color than most, and the curtains reminded me of our house in Calgary. As soon as we pulled up, we saw Milo and Mary standing in the doorway smiling. Milo had a broad smile and twinkly eyes. He wasn't very tall, but he looked really strong, like one of those strongmen in the circus. He had a big round chest and arms, and a small waist and skinny legs.

I had never seen Mary without her uniform on. She had her hair down, and it was kind of wavy, and fell to her shoulders. She had a bright pair of pants on, and a flowered top in the same colors. She wore glasses, and looked taller than Milo. She smiled at us, and told us to come in because it was cold, and as we walked up the driveway, I thought I felt a few stinging, frosty snowflakes blow against my cheeks.

Once we were inside, and our coats were hung up on the hall rack, Dad introduced Mom to both of our hosts. Mary gave Mom a hug and said that she had heard a lot about her, and Milo shook her hand and said that it was nice to meet her. Mom looked kind of surprised, and looked at Dad, who said "Here, Lola, sit down," as Milo motioned everyone over to the couch.

Milo took a look at me, and reached out his hand to shake mine—he said that Mary had told him that I looked just like my dad, and he could see it now. Mary said over her shoulder that the girls at the café had started calling me "Little-Sam," when I came to the café a couple of times a week to have lunch with Dad and some of his business friends. The booth would usually be full—with Dad and two or three other guys who all knew my name, and he would get one of them to move over so I could sit beside him. Dad would help me take off my parka, pulling one sleeve down so I could get my arm out, and ask me what I wanted for lunch as Mary came over with a glass of water or pop.

Once we were settled on the couch I began to notice how good it smelled in the house. Not Baba's kitchen good... sort of spicy and garlic-y. Mary said that Milo did all the cooking because she worked around food all day, and Milo was from a country in Europe that had an unpronounceable name and was an excellent cook, and had cooked for many years in the army and in work-camps up north. After more small talk—Mary and Mom, Milo and Dad—Milo stood up and said that dinner was ready, and we should have a seat at the table.

147

We all got up and walked a few steps into a small dining room with lots of pictures on the wall with a china cabinet in the corner. Mary's dishes were beautiful, with flowers around the rim, and Milo said that the dishes were his mother's, and he couldn't believe that they'd made it all the way to Yellowknife in one piece! We sat down, and Mary poured everyone except me some red wine, and brought me over a diet Pepsi just like at the café. Milo brought out a big pot filled with some kind of stew, and we ate it with the big chunks of what looked like homemade bread. The stew was filled with meat and carrots and potatoes, and Dad ate like he had never eaten food before. Even Mom had a second helping.

Mom, Dad, and Milo chatted at one end of the table, while Mary asked me about school and if I had made some friends yet. I told her that I liked school and my teacher, and was probably going to join Brownies and maybe go camping. Mary asked me if I knew where the ice skating rink was, and if I knew how to skate. I told her that Dad had taught me at the indoor rink at the Calgary Winter Club… especially the part about him pushing me over so that I could learn how to get up! Mary said that the ice rink was brand new and was very nice, and that she had done a lot of skating when she was young and lived somewhere in northern BC. She said that she didn't have any children, and that her first husband had died, and Milo didn't want any, and anyway she was too old for all of that now…

After dinner, we all went back to the couch, and Milo gave Mom and Dad some special liquor in tiny little glasses, and after a while Mom and Dad were both looking tired, so Dad said we should be going.

There were a few more hugs at the door, and then Mary went into another room and came back carrying what looked like a brand-new pair of ladies' ice skates. They were so white…and the toe pick was so sharp…I was sure that she was going to ask me to go skating with her so she could break them in. I didn't have ice skates. We rented a pair at the Winter Club when I was learning, and would have probably bought me a pair this winter if we hadn't left Calgary and our Winter Club membership—along with our house—behind.

Mary asked me what size feet I had. I looked down at my boots and tried to remember, and Mom said I had big feet like Dad and was already wearing a size eight. Mary said that these skates were a size seven and a half or eight, and that she didn't have time to skate any more, as she was always working—and besides, if she fell she might break a hip! So if I wanted them, I could have them.

I looked up from my boots and couldn't believe what I was hearing. I looked at Mary and then at Mom, and Mom asked if I wanted them. I nodded, and Mom said that they looked brand new, and asked if we could give her some money for them, and Mary shook her head. "No," she said. "Absolutely not, they were just lying around in a box waiting for someone to use them." And as she was saying that, she draped the knotted laces over one of my shoulders so that one skate was lying on my stomach and the other on my back and gave both my shoulders a squeeze. I threw my arms around her waist and squeezed her back, and when I looked up at her she was smiling, and her eyes were shining. She told me to enjoy the skates, and she would see me next week at the café for lunch.

On the car ride home, every time we went under a street light, the beam of light would catch the shining skate blade or the white of the skate boot, and while Mom and Dad talked about the evening in the front seat, I couldn't stop looking at my new skates.

MY NEW TEACHER

SEPTEMBER TURNED TO October, and I was enjoying all that school had to offer. I was getting used to the routine of school, recess, lunch, recess, home. I was now taking books out of the school library—the school librarian and my homeroom teacher were both very kind and smart. I was learning a lot about history and English, and starting to learn a few words in French.

My homeroom is where all our classes took place, and our desks were arranged in rows facing the huge chalkboard. One wall was solid and was papered with students' work, posters for school events, inspirational phrases, and maps. There were no back or side walls; we listened to our teacher teach us in a lower voice, and when we raised our hand to answer a question, our voices were lower as well.

I found the school day much more serene than my days in North Haven Elementary, where it felt like everyone was constantly screaming or running. My class probably consisted of 15 to 20 students, in three or four rows of five desks. As the months went on our teacher learned more about us, and one day as class was ending for the day, she asked to speak with me.

She said that we were going to start a module on public speaking, and we were going to each write a short speech, memorize the speech the best we could, and do the speech in front of the class.

She told me that I would be a great public speaker, and that I should start thinking about topics I would like to speak on. She also said that if I liked, I could come over to her house on Saturday, and we could do some work together, as she had a couple of books she thought that I might like to read. I was excited at the prospect and said that I would come over on Saturday with a couple of topics.

Over the next few Saturdays I visited my teacher's house, and her house reminded me of our school. It was clean and white, with a bit of light wood furniture. She listened to classical music on CBC radio, and the sound echoed through the space—sounds I had never heard before. Violins and clarinets, and cellos. We would sit at her kitchen table and talk, and she would leave me alone to write, and then would come back and we would talk some more. She would make me a sandwich for lunch, and have fruit cut up on a plate, and when a few hours had passed, I would put on my parka and go back home. It was about a 30-minute walk from her place to the bakery.

There had already been a couple of snowfalls, and like in Calgary it felt like the wind blew constantly. In Calgary the bad wind was the north wind, and as I was now living in the actual North, I couldn't seem to figure out where the wind was coming from. Did they call it the north-north wind? I was grateful for the large hood on my parka trimmed with some sort of real fur, that was supposed to prevent the fur from sticking to your face in the cold.

When I got closer to the Bay, I knew the bakery was right around the corner—and as was my habit now that the temperature had dropped, I cut through the Bay, looking at all the merchandise I passed that was located in the center aisle. Clothing, housewares, shoes, small appliances... and when I got to the door, I could see the white fence, and I knew that once I was over that, I had about 20 steps into the back storeroom of the bakery. A quick glance and "Hi," to Dad, Lily and Mr. Xavier, then up the dark stairs to the quiet apartment. Mom would be sleeping or smoking in her chair, with the TV on low, maybe tuned to news. As it was Saturday, and not a weekday, there was no Dad snoozing on the couch half-watching *The Edge of Night* on the TV.

TROUBLE

OCTOBER TURNED TO November and I still hadn't made any real friends, so my teacher and the library were my support at school. On the weekends I read or helped out in the bakery, and in my walks discovered that Yellowknife had a movie theater. Saturday matinees were the only movies I had ever seen in Calgary. I think Bambi and Dumbo were the choices for my age at that time, but the matinees in Yellowknife were more "mature." I used to call the movie theater on Saturday morning to listen to the recording of what was playing and decide whether or not I was going to pay the one or two dollars to sit in the dark for a few hours.

I remember two matinees from that winter. In fact, all these years later, I wish I could forget… One Saturday the featured film was called *The Deadly Bees*. Listening to the recording, I couldn't quite figure out what that meant. It was the same as when David used to take me to the A&W Drive-In in Calgary. We always tried to park the car as near to the front as possible, and I would always order the root beer in the tiny frosty mug to go with my burger and fries, and I would always read the sentence printed on the window on the front of the restaurant: *Turn on lights for service.* I always thought— *what lights? What's "service?"*

But back to the bees. On the recording, I thought maybe they were talking about a family of criminals with the last name Bee. Or maybe the word deadly referred to pretty girls, like Barbie, or a really funny family. At the appointed time, I put on my parka and told Mom that I was going to the movies. At the theater, I paid little to no attention to the movie poster, and headed over to the concession stand. I bought a square cardboard package of Glosette chocolate-covered raisins and made my way into the theater to find a good seat.

I was practically the only one in there, so I sat right in the middle as the lights dimmed and the previews started. The theater probably had about 100 seats, and they were upholstered in a sort of burgundy burnout velvet... and like the rest of the buildings in Yellowknife, looked like something from another decade.

I settled myself into my seat. As it was minus something or another outside, the theater was a little chilly, I kept my parka on, but I took off my mittens so I could more easily eat my chocolate raisins. Before I knew it, the previews were over and the movie started.

I should have known by the music that this movie may not have been for me. The first scene had a lovely woman in a yellow dress standing in a field, with classical-type music playing, and I thought, *OK, I wonder what's going to happen?* And as I was putting my first chocolate-covered raisin in my mouth, all of a sudden the carnage on the screen began.

It started with one or two bees buzzing around the pretty woman, who carelessly swatted them away. As the music became louder, and the sky turned from blue to a sort of ominous gray, the poor woman was swarmed by bees. They were stinging her about a million times, all over her face and arms, and she was screaming and swatting until she fell over in the field—obviously dead—and the bees covered her entire body, obscuring her pretty yellow dress. The music turned back to lovely birds singing, while the camera panned back up to the lovely blue sky.

When I could blink my eyes again, I realized that the chocolate-covered raisin in my mouth was still there, but the chocolate had melted and the raisin sat between my cheek and my teeth because for the past three minutes, in my terror, I had forgotten to chew.

The movie continued in another setting—someone's house, or another backyard, maybe, and I thought maybe the worst was over. I was hanging on to the armrest with one hand and my box of Glosettes with the other, and I slowly relaxed my grip of both and started to breathe normally.

I looked around the theater to see if the other patrons were as shocked by the last scene as I had been, and a couple of couples were laughing and snuggling, and the other couple of singles like me were acting like nothing had happened. I wish I could say that the bees did not return, but they did, and a variety of people were swarmed and stung... and after 90 minutes or so, the screen turned to black.

When the movie was over, I realized that not only had I sweated all the way through my heavy parka, but that my hand that was holding the raisins had tightened to the point where the package was mangled and the chocolate had melted into my hand and onto my parka. I hadn't moved a muscle or eaten a raisin for the entire show.

As people got up to leave, I tried to get up, but was extremely stiff because every muscle in my body been clenched. I needed to relax enough for me to rise out of my seat... all I could think of was getting out of there before the next showing. I threw the destroyed box of raisins into the trash as I left, and tried to wipe the now-dried chocolate stain off my nearly new parka. It was snowing when I left the theater, and as it was 2 p.m. in November the sun was very low in the sky. I was pretty shook up, as I kept thinking about the pretty girl in the yellow dress getting stung to death and how scared she must have been, out there in the field all alone...

At the beginning of December it was dark all day long. I would wake up in the dark. Walk to school in the dark and the cold, and at recess, around 10:30 a.m., the sun would start to rise a little, but by lunchtime it would be as dark as midnight again. It was more difficult to keep everyone quiet as we walked from classroom to classroom, as Christmas decorations were going up around the school. Christmas-type projects were being created to decorate the school and bring home to our families.

One day, our teacher had to leave us alone while she attended to some other school business. We were supposed to stay at our desks and read until she got back. I have no idea what possessed me, but I decided to stand up and announce to my classmates that I thought that we should, as a group, take the huge stack of individual projects we were working on—that looked like square cardboard box-things—and move them from where they were stacked against the wall and pile them on the ledge where there was no wall but was instead our view of the open staircase going down to the office and the front door. To my surprise, they agreed, and we started carefully and quietly, whispering to each other as we decided how everything was going to stack, hoping against hope that none or all of the boxes fell off the ledge and down the stairs.

After about 15 minutes, we all stood back and admired our handiwork. The stack looked even and stable, and our classroom had turned into a version of a fort, as we had constructed a three-foot wall where there had been none. We were still milling around whispering when our teacher came back.

This was my homeroom teacher, who had had me over to her house on Saturdays to read and study and had been so kind. This version of my teacher was one I had never seen before. She was furious and spitting mad and demanded to know whose idea it had been to move our projects. When no one named a culprit, she insisted that we move them back to where they were immediately, in silence, and after the task was complete return to our desks, fold our hands over our desks and put our heads down.

My heart was pounding, and I felt sick, sure that someone would name me as the instigator—thinking that if they couldn't remember my name, they would identify me as "that girl from Calgary." I laid my head face down in my arms, and after a few minutes, I turned my head to the left, and found myself staring into the blue eyes of a big kid with thick red hair. I must have looked worried, but he just smirked and rolled his eyes.

No one told on me that day at school. As a class we were punished in some way, but I was not singled out. The red-haired kid's name was Doug, and he was my first friend in Yellowknife.

MIDDAY STARS, BLACK DOGS, AND DOUG

I WAS BORN in Winnipeg, at the end of January in a snowstorm. I had lived nearly ten years of my life in northwest Calgary. So when I think about winters in Yellowknife, I think about how much fun they were.

Doug and I started hanging out that first winter. I mostly talked incessantly about Calgary, and my family, and more about Calgary, but as the days passed I found out that he had a couple of brothers and he lived in a house near the school. And the fact I found the most fascinating was that this big kid with red hair and blue eyes was born in Tuktoyaktuk! His dad was a professor, or a scientist, or (like many of the people who ended up working in Yellowknife) worked for the government. He didn't seem too impressed that I had moved all the way from Calgary or that I had a beautiful cat, but the fact that my dad was a baker, he was impressed by that.

It was dark nearly all the time at that point. The snow was pretty deep, and if people could drive to get from point A to point B, they did. I remember the wind and the blowing snow, and on clear days and nights, the beautiful deep navy of a sky filled with stars. The North Star in Yellowknife seemed to me as bright as the moon, and when the moon was up and the sky was clear, it was like a spotlight that followed me wherever I walked.

I used to stop at crosswalks on my way to and from school or Doug's, and I was constantly turning my head to avoid the wind blowing my hood off. I would occasionally see another lone walker like myself far in the distance, head bent down against the wind, big boots crunching in the snow, and to me it looked like a photograph. The flatness. The brightness of the dark night sky, the lone figure. The snow so bright against the dark, glittering like a million diamonds on the ground, or as it whipped by your face in a sheet of sheer white glitter.

There was a limit to how cold it would have to be before school was closed. As a country we were on the cusp of adopting the metric system, but the number I recall was minus 50 Fahrenheit. Walking to school in the morning at minus 48 or 49 was something that happened, but my parka was warm, and so were my boots. There was something so primal in the way that I needed to get to school. In the morning, the Bay was closed, so no cutting through for warmth was possible—so I walked the distance outdoors. On the occasion that the temperature dropped to those dangerous levels, I just kept my destination in focus.

I learned to spot the signs of frostbite in Yellowknife. Mr. Xavier told me what to look for. Little white bumps on my cheeks or tingling and numbness and finally pain—real pain—in my fingers and toes. He knew my route to school and told me to warm up in the high school if I got really cold. Dad would glance my way some mornings as I headed out through the bakery back door, and tell me to do my coat up and hold my hood closed if the wind was really howling. I never did get frostbite, although I remember that my rosy cheeks lasted through the entire winter. My face was always chapped by the wind. I guess I was on my way to becoming a northerner.

Doug's house was a wonder. The first time he invited me over, I was surprised that we had to walk up a little hill to get to it. It kind of reminded me of Calgary. The house had a steep driveway, and we scrabbled up the incline on what must have been the front lawn, trying to step in the tracks of the others in the household who had reached the front door in the same way. He swung the door open—no one locked their doors in Yellowknife—and he said that his mom and dad were at work, and yelled his brothers' names (to no answer). Like me, he had older brothers, six or seven years older. I was going to launch into a story about my brothers, and that he would get to meet them when they joined us in Yellowknife—maybe this spring—but I never got the words out.

My attention was captured by the sight of the biggest, blackest dog I had ever seen in my life, standing at the top of the staircase. The dog's head, from my angle at the bottom of the stairs, looked like it filled the space from wall to wall. He had eyes as black as his fur, just like a raven, and when we locked eyes, he let out a throaty, low *woof.*

Doug must have seen the look on my face, and he pulled my arm so I would move out of the small entryway into a smallish room to the right and shouted in the dog's direction, "Come on!" And the enormous dog, *and* another dog that looked like his twin, came thundering down the stairs and out the open door.

He told me their names and told me that they were Newfoundland dogs, or they were from Newfoundland, or something like that, and the two of them ran around the front yard like wild creatures so grateful for the fresh air and the chance to relieve themselves. They barked at each other, and chased each other, and a couple of times raised themselves up to nip at each others' heads, and I stood there amazed at the show they were putting on.

Doug said that he was going to go outside and take them up the side of the house to the fenced backyard, and told me that they could play outside until after supper, as they both had dog houses they could stay warm in... but that they always slept in the house at night. As Doug ran out the front door yelling the dogs' names, and they both followed him around the side of the house, I looked around the small basement room I was standing in.

The first thing I noticed was a glowing aquarium that seemed to be built into the rock wall, and the enormous dark gray fish swimming back and forth in the tank. The rock was the same kind of rock that surrounded Yellowknife, and was present in the cellar room where we kept the flour in the bakery. I heard the front door slam, and Doug said "It's a miniature shark," and said he was going upstairs to get something to eat, and did I want something?

I said sure, and he ran up the stairs, and came back in a few minutes with a piece of bread with peanut butter and jam. One for him, and one for me. We sat down and ate our bread, and he told me about his family and his brothers, and a couple of kids in the neighborhood that he hung around with. Doug asked me if I could skate, and had I ever been sledding on a Krazy Karpet, or had I ever ridden on a snowmobile? I said yes to skating and no to the other two, and he said that I should come to the free skate at the arena this Saturday, and maybe that we could go sledding one day after school because the hill behind his house was really steep. His family had two snowmobiles, Doug told me, and when it wasn't so cold they would drive out to the bush and ride through the trails near Prelude Lake. He said that I could wear his mom's snowmobile suit if I wanted to come.

As I was considering what all this activity would mean to my up to then non existent social-life, I agreed to everything (especially the free skate on Saturday) and started to tell him about my brand-new skates. Just then, the front door burst open and two people came in and pulled down their hoods, unzipped their parkas and hung them on the hooks in the entry. Doug said hi, and introduced me to his two brothers, who (although taller) had the same eyes, and same thick red hair. They said hi, and asked if he had let the dogs out, and if he had started supper.

I got up and put on my parka, as I couldn't remember how long I had been there, and told Doug that I would see him tomorrow at school. One of his brothers bent down to help me with my parka zipper and asked me where I lived, and if my mom or dad was picking me up. I told them I lived above the bakery downtown, put up my hood, and said it was OK. I would walk.

Puss-Puss and the Ravens

PUSS-PUSS WAS DEFINITELY an indoor cat when we lived in Calgary. In Yellowknife, she had free rein of the apartment—and as I was to learn later, made regular midnight forays down to the cellar. In the summer, she used to slink out the bedroom window whenever she liked, as the balcony gave her some roaming room and a bit of fresh air.

In the winter, the roof of the bakery addition was piled high with snow, and if she meowed at the window I would attempt to crank it open—sometimes needing a cup of hot water from the bathroom to melt the ice that had sealed it shut. Puss-Puss would daintily step out onto the top of the snow, barely a few inches down. She was fluffy, but quite thin underneath, so she could tip-toe along the drifts, rarely breaking through, her legs nowhere near the balcony floor.

She was mostly white, with large patches of brown and black, and the ravens who sat on the telephone wires in the alley all day long always took notice when she decided to venture out on a day that wasn't too frigid or too windy. (She didn't seem to mind the cold, but she absolutely hated the wind.)

Puss-Puss was blessed with magnificent whiskers, and I believe she used them to sense danger. She would stay close to the building, sort of creeping slowly up and down on the drifted snow. The other three sides of the balcony were open, no railing, no shelter at all, so she was completely exposed, should she decide to walk the entire perimeter.

The ravens, usually in packs of three or four, would sit on the wires, and turn their heads her way when they spotted her on the roof. They would caw and click their tongues, and on the occasion where she let out a plaintive meow, I swear a few times those ravens meowed right back.

The ravens were the most remarkable birds I had ever encountered. They were different than the magpies in Calgary, which would make a ton of noise but seemed sort of silly and brainless. I used to sit at my window whenever she was outside and watch. There was nothing I could do, in case the ravens decided to do her harm, but my thought was that at least I could give a shout to warn her.

From the moment Puss-Puss's paw emerged from the open window, followed by paw number two and, little by little, the rest of her, Puss-Puss and those ravens never took their eyes off one another. The routine was the same every time, and in a funny way, I think she enjoyed the sport. One by one, the ravens would casually step off the wire, spread their huge wings, and just before hitting the ground, swoop up with a tremendous beating of their wings. Then the three or four of them would fly high up into the dark blue sky and start to circle, slowly but deliberately. She would position herself half a foot from the window on the open snow, facing the alley, her head up, watching for the first one to drop in. And drop they would: one at a time, one after the other, heads down, wings spread, and talons out. The only sound was the sound of the wind in their wings as they swooped and tried to grab a little scrap of fur or flesh.

She was ready, head up until the last moment, when she would lay her head down in the snow and flatten herself—like a sheet of paper, white and black and brown—against the bright, glittering snow. The first time I heard the swoop of wings and turned my head to see the next raven perform his dive, I let out a little scream, realizing that not only could I not climb out the window or up the oil barrel to save her, but that it was all my fault that she was out there alone and exposed in the first place. But after a few times, I realized that she was holding her own, only occasionally losing a clump of fur in the feline/avian battle.

This day, no fur was lost, and as usual, when the third raven was taking his position in the circle high in the sky, she would calmly lift her head to view her predators. She lifted herself up carefully off the hard, crusty snow, and only then would she take her eyes off the birds and turn her head back towards the window.

I would see two white paws on the window sill, and with a delicate slink, she would slide back onto my room, hop onto the bed, and settle down for her nightly cleaning. After I cranked the window shut, I would look over at her in amazement, and she would turn her head my way and give me a little squeak, as if to say, "How did I do?"

ICE AND SNOW

ON SATURDAY MORNINGS, for the remainder of the winter, I ate breakfast, got dressed, threw my beautiful skates over my shoulder, and headed downstairs. I would always stop at the café to see if Mary was working, to let her know that not only did I now have a new friend to go skating with, but that I was going to put her generous gift to good use.

Mary always looked so pleased to see me. She asked me about school, and sometimes reached deep into her front apron pocket for some change to give me—telling me to buy myself a hot chocolate "on her," with a wink and a smile. I waved to her as I pushed open the front door and walked over to the rink.

The free skate was in full swing when I arrived that first Saturday. I spotted Doug right away, as a blur of red hair flew around the rink. I was a little apprehensive when I saw how fast everyone was skating, but as I was walking over to the bench to sit and lace up my skates, he appeared and skidded to a stop, spraying me with ice. He said a couple of his friends were here, and he'd see me later, and was gone. I wondered why he hadn't mentioned "other friends" and wondered if they were from school.

I laced up my skates, good and tight, pulled down my jeans over the tops of my skates—almost a shame to hide the beautiful whiteness—and stepped onto the ice. The music was blaring, and the place was packed. Little kids hanging onto their parents, girls in the middle jumping and spinning, boys skating like mad fiends playing tag and diving onto the ice surface to avoid being "it," and a few couples holding hands and trying to stay together and upright while avoiding the chaos.

I took a couple of steps and started to glide, trying to keep my ankles straight and not to lean forward too far on my toe picks, which would result in an embarrassing face-plant. I was trying to get the feel of skating again, without falling and/or running into someone else, when someone sped towards me and grabbed my arm. It was Doug, and he was pulling me out of the round and round crowd into the less crowded middle, towards two other boys and a girl.

He introduced me to Scott and Billy—both neighbors, both a year older—and Gillian, a girl who had just moved to Yellowknife, whose dad worked with Doug's dad. We all said hi, and Doug started talking to them, telling them that my dad was a baker, and I lived downtown, and that we were in the same class and that I had moved to Yellowknife from Calgary. Then he asked me if I knew how to skate backwards, and I said no, and he said he would teach me. The other three watched as he demonstrated in his hockey skates, and Doug told me to watch my toe picks and that I would have to push out, not straight back. As the music played and the people skated and laughed, fell, and got up, somehow, I learned to skate backwards.

Christmas was coming, but as we didn't really have any money for presents (nor was there really anyplace to shop), I was surprised to come home from school one day to see a small silver tinsel-tree set up on a table in our living room. I saw Puss-Puss sitting on the floor admiring it (or scheming how to knock it over), and Mom said that we could put up some Christmas lights as well because she thought there was a box in the spare room from Calgary. I found them, and we hung them on the front windows, and turned them on, and they gave off a pretty glow against the dark blue carpet and the bright orange fireplace.

Dad came upstairs to have a look and told me that as it was holiday time, to be careful crossing the streets on the way home from school—people had started going to Christmas parties, and they might be driving drunk and might not see me. A kid got hit by a car and died that morning as the person was still drunk from the night before. They were driving their car home from a house party and ran right over the kid and kept going. I was trying to not imagine that poor kid lying on the ground in the snow dying, and so I nodded OK. I tried to imagine being so drunk that you wouldn't even notice what was on the road, first thing in the morning—and then tried not to imagine it.

School was winding down, and we were all a little more rambunctious than usual. One day at school, a kid in my class came in after an absence I hadn't even noticed. He was hard not to notice now. One side of his face was banged up, complete with a bloody eyeball and a black eye. His arm was in a sling, and his wrist in a cast. He wasn't a big kid, and when all the boys crowded around him to pat him on the back or check out his eye or his cast, he looked tiny.

Our teacher had all of us sit, except the kid, who stood up at the front of the class near her. She pulled her chair around so he could sit, and she told us that there had been an accident over the weekend, and the kid wanted to tell us about it so he wouldn't have to tell the story 20 times.

The kid and his dad had gone out hunting. The weather was pretty clear, and the kid's dad was an experienced hunter, so they drove out into the bush and took their snowmobile out to look for a caribou. After a couple of hours, when it started to get a little light and they hadn't had any luck, they decided to head back to the truck.

They heard and smelled something in the trees a mile or so from the snowmobile, so the kid's dad got the rifle ready, and he sat the kid at the front of the snowmobile and started it up, and told the kid if anything happened he was supposed to follow the tracks back to the truck.

Before he could finish the sentence, a huge polar bear came running out of the trees, straight at them, and the kid's dad shot twice but the bear kept running. The kid's dad told him to go, while he tried to re-load the gun, but the polar bear grabbed him and shook him and threw him over his head. The kid screamed, and the polar bear looked over, and with one swipe knocked him off the snowmobile—and the kid must have lost consciousness.

When he woke up, the polar bear was gone, and his dad's half-eaten body was lying in the snow. At this point in the story, the kid started to wipe his eyes, and I realized that some of us had been holding our breaths—a bunch of kids started gasping for air, and a couple of girls started crying, and I looked over at Doug and his eyes were as big as saucers. The teacher crouched down in front of the kid with a tissue, and told him he could stop if he wanted to, but after a couple of minutes, he started talking again in a low voice.

When he came to, the kid told us, the bear had gone, and the snowmobile was still running, and he knew that he needed to get back to their truck before the snowmobile ran out of gas. He didn't want to leave what was left of his dad's body out in the bush, as his mom would want to bury him, so he drove the snowmobile over the blood-red snow and pulled the body onto the back of the snowmobile, and turned it around. He followed the bobbing headlight back through the woods until he saw their truck. He turned the snowmobile off, and got into the truck and started it up—his dad always left the keys in the truck, as he didn't want to take them with him just in case they fell out of his pocket, and they were lost in the snow. The kid, now feeling quite lightheaded, turned on the CB radio and called for help on the channel reserved for emergencies, and sat in the truck with a couple of blankets pulled tight around him and waited for help.

When he was finished the story, the kid started to cry again, and all of us sat in our seats stunned and in shock. One by one, we walked to the front of the class, and hugged each other and the teacher and the poor kid.

After a little while, the teacher said that it was time for recess, but if we wanted, we could just go home...

THE BOYS

THE SPRING BROUGHT a huge snowmelt, which turned the entire town into a lake. I traded my cool fake suede and sherpa boots for gum boots, like everyone did, and sloshed through the icy, slushy water to school and back.

I came home one day to David and Richard standing in the bakery talking to Dad. When I walked in the back door and past the big mixer on the floor, the three of them turned and stared at me like they had seen a ghost. Richard said something charming about how fat I had gotten, and David made some comment about my long hair and dirty parka, and Dad told them to shut up and listen to him.

They were old now. David 24, Richard 26. In the year and a half since I had seen them last they had changed into men. Sort of snarly, dismissive, grown men who wanted nothing to do with a little sister. I hated how they were when they were together, and it got worse when they were together with Dad. Clearly the days were gone when I had been a novelty, somewhat cute, possibly huggable or small enough to lift up and carry around.

When I was a little kid, my natural inclination when I saw any one of my family was to raise my arms and hope that someone would pick me up. The look I got from the two of them that day, complete with nasty comments about my appearance, made me realize that those early days of kindness and affection were well and truly gone… and I had better get used to it.

I was surprised to see them, and I must have said something stupid, like "hi," and David—still looking at me like he barely recognized the short, stocky girl in front of him with the long dark hair—screwed up his face and said, "hi," back, in a high, sarcastic, sing-song voice, and with a sneer turned his back to me to face Dad and his brother.

I turned the corner and walked up the stairs to see Mom. I thought that maybe she would be pleased that "her boys" were here, and that I would walk in and see her up out of her chair, with a smile on the face that had been blank and unseeing for the past 18 months. But as I turned to face the living room and watched her hand, holding a cigarette, move slowly up and down from her lips to the ashtray, I knew that nothing had changed. I said I was home, and she asked if I had seen the boys, and I said I had, and looked around at the suitcases outside what had been the empty room beside mine.

There was a huge pile of laundry sitting on the floor in front of the washing machine. As I walked to my room, rubber boots squeaking on the linoleum tiles, Mom said that I should put a load of laundry in, and we would have Chinese food from the café for dinner.

I thought that may have been the longest sentence she had spoken to me since we had arrived in Yellowknife.

Puss-Puss was sitting on my bed looking wide-eyed and distressed—clearly unhappy with our new residents, and I thought that they had probably, one by one come into my room, and *pssspssed* her in an aggressive way, scaring her. I could feel that they had been in my room, each of them separately, to have a look around.

Richard hadn't lived at our house in Calgary since I was six years old, and had visited very infrequently, as he and Dad and David did not get along. David had lived with us until he got married, minus his stay in Spy Hill Jail, and of the two of them, if I was forced to pick the lesser of two evils, he was my choice.

On the high dresser in the corner of my room, I spotted a turn-table, and propped against the receiver underneath (which had a tape deck and a radio) what looked like a new album, still in the plastic. The cover was like a tie-dyed t-shirt, all purples, and reds and yellows, with two words—*Sound Explosion*—in fat, rounded letters. I knew it was from David, and I was glad he had not forgotten me, despite the show he had put on 5 minutes ago downstairs in the bakery. Pretending he wasn't at all glad to see me or had missed me. Oh no, in front of Dad or Richard, shows of affection or kindness would be considered signs of weakness and would not be tolerated.

The turntable and receiver were plugged in, and I spotted one speaker on my little makeup table, and another one in front of the window, and realized that he must have taken the time to look around my room, find the plugs, connect the speaker wire to the speakers, and set them up for maximum stereo sound. I checked to see that there was a needle in the turntable arm, and it looked like he had put in a brand-new one.

He had probably taken a few minutes to have a chat with Puss-Puss, and may have even sat on my bed and given her a good scratch with his rough hands. The fingernails on David's hands were bitten as far down as they could go, and when he had finished chewing those, he had started on the skin around the cuticles, which if I remembered were usually ragged and scabby in places. She would have remembered how he smelled, and would have probably even purred a little in greeting.

I carefully took the album over to the bed, and had a good look, especially the back, for the song list. The songs were new to me, but some of the artists were familiar: The Stampeders, Blood, Sweat and Tears, Lighthouse... I couldn't wait to play it, but I would wait to thank him, and let him tell me all about the stereo set up—and I didn't want to touch anything, just in case the stereo was in my room, but it was *his*, in which case, I wouldn't be allowed to touch it.

In our small garage in Calgary, there were some album covers nailed to one wall. I knew from the kind of music that was played in David's car which albums were his. He liked any kind of rock music, and he liked to play it loud. As I spent most of my time in his car, my taste was formed by him. From fried eggs to cinnamon toast to A&W, I liked what he liked, and that included music… and the volume the music was played at.

As I sat on the bed turning the brand-new album over and over, reading every word, including the sentences regarding copyright, I wondered how this new version of our family was going to work.

But before I could think much about it, I heard someone clomping up the stairs in their cowboy boots, the door was flung open and I heard David shout for Mom and then me, and I walked out of my room holding the album, still in my coat and boots.

He asked me if I liked the album, and told me to go down the street to buy him a case of Coke, while he dug around in the pocket of his leather jacket for some money. I turned and placed the album gently on the bed, and smiled to myself, thinking that maybe things were going to get better.

Friendships

SPRING WAS A long season with a little more daylight, but snow and cold persisted, so did the dark. I continued to hang out at Doug's place, but there were usually four of us now on outings: Doug, Scott, Gillian, and me. As the weather got nicer, and the snow melted from a few feet high to perhaps a foot high, there were still lots of winter things to do. Doug loved to grab his Krazy Karpet after school and invite me over to hike up the huge hill behind his house.

The routine was the same: Open the front door and step aside to let the giant black monster dogs out. Persuade the dogs to follow him into the chain-linked enclosure/backyard. Then climb further up the hill, with the dogs barking and playing, threatening to jump over the fence to join us as we positioned our Krazy Karpets on one of the two tracks down the mini-mountain to the road below. At this time of year, the smooth rock was poking through in patches, and the road at the bottom was filled with huge lakes of icy water. The aim was to avoid the rocks, make the required turns, and slide onto the dryer part of the street, flattening yourself like Puss-Puss on the bakery roof while you slid underneath the red pickup truck parked at the bottom of the hill.

Doug was like a military commander, standing at the top of the hill and using his hands to demonstrate what was needed for a safe, dry slide to the bottom. The traffic was minimal, so getting hit by a car as you slid out from underneath the pickup truck was only a slim possibility. However, should the slider hear a shout from the top of the hill—the all-familiar "Car!"—it was time for evasive action. The tactic was to grab onto some piece of the truck undercarriage, sacrifice the Krazy Karpet to the oncoming vehicle, tuck your legs under the truck to avoid ankles and feet (and in Doug's case, legs) being run over, and live to slide another day.

By the end of the spring, I could have piloted that Krazy Karpet blindfolded, and only once did I hear the word "Car" shouted with a sense of urgency. Luckily when the driver of the car saw the bright red Krazy Karpet slide under the red pickup truck they slammed on their brakes and stopped the car. They got out to scream at Doug, who was standing at the top of the hill, and then leaned down to see me under the truck. They pulled me out by one leg, helped me get up, and screamed at me, too. The woman demanded to know where we lived, and wanted to speak to our parents, and we explained that our parents were at work, as like me, Doug seemed to live a pretty "feral" life, with his only supervision being his two brothers on occasion.

After the poor woman calmed down, she made me promise that we would stop sliding into the street, and as I looked extremely sorry and told her that we would, she got back in her car and drove away.

Doug motioned for me to join him at the top of the hill, and as I was climbing I ran into Scott, who was climbing up from his backyard, with his yellow Krazy Karpet under his arm.

Gillian was a friend of Doug's, but she and I spent time together over the long winter. She lived in a nice house, and she had an older brother and a younger sister. Her parents spoke with an accent—I believe they were from South Africa—and Gillian said that in her dad's work with the government they had lived all over the world. Before coming to Yellowknife, they had lived in the Mariana Islands, and she still had a tan from living there for a few years. I asked her if she was OK with moving around so much, and she said that it was fun to live in different places, and she even thought Yellowknife was cool!

I took the opportunity to launch into the incredibly sad story of Dad going bankrupt and Mom being depressed and our terrible living conditions compared to the "palace" that was my childhood home on Norquay Drive. I think I might have even squeezed out a tear or two.

When I was done, Gillian said that she thought that my circumstances might get better now that my brothers had arrived, and maybe I would be moving somewhere better soon. Then she asked me if I wanted to go to a movie matinee.

I had not set foot in that theater since the bee-movie sting-fest that left me terrified and smeared with chocolate, but she was a new, older friend, and I didn't want to sound like a baby, so I said sure. We walked down to the movie theater and there on the marquee was the feature, in huge letters with at least three exclamation points—*WICKED WICKED!!!*

I was feeling sick already, as I knew that there was no misinterpreting the title this time. We bought a drink and a popcorn to share and found a couple of seats, middle-center. Unlike my last experience, the theater was packed with kids, and it seemed like we had just sat down when the lights dimmed and the previews began. One of the previews was for the movie we were there to see, so I was lucky to learn a little more about how scared I was soon to be!

The movie was filmed with something called a "split screen" so while something quite normal was happening on in the left screen, the right screen would have someone running for their life or being stabbed 50 times with the blood running down the screen. I thought that I would try to concentrate on the "normal" screen, and I would try not to choke on my pop or spill the popcorn when something really bad happened that would cause me to jump. Except for the lead actor—who was very nice-looking, with brilliant blue eyes— the movie was as terrifying as it was billed.

Gillian laughed through most of it, and the screams and moans from the audience were a sort of signal whether or not I could open my eyes. It was definitely my first slasher film, and as I recall, my last! As we were walking out, I vowed again never to set foot in that theater.

THE ALLEY

IT WAS DARK when we got out, and we went our separate ways with a wave once we were out on the sidewalk. I walked with some of the crowd for a bit, re-playing some of the more gruesome scenes every time I closed my eyes, until I realized I had walked past Marshall Wells and was standing on The Tog Shop corner. I thought that it would be safer for me to walk down the sidewalk in front of the bakery and cut through the alley in between the bakery and the Gold Range Hotel.

I got to the entrance to the narrow alley in between the two buildings, trying to not look at or talk to the crowd (of mostly men) gathered outside the door of the hotel bar, who were mostly drunk and smoking and laughing. I always ran down the alley, especially after dark, as there was a vent about 6 feet up the wall of the hotel that sucked the smoke out of the bar, and when it was cold, the hot smoky air from the bar mixed with the cold air in the alley created a sort of fog bank. I thought of going around the other side, and into the bakery through the back screen door—but it was cold, and the alley was faster.

As usual, I took a bit of a runner's stance, and started to run. It usually took me about 5 seconds to run the length of the alley, but almost as soon as I started running, I tripped over someone who was sprawled on the ground. I banged my head on the ground, and as I was starting to get up, someone grabbed me and sort of growled at me, and all I could smell was liquor.

I screamed, and they put their hand over my mouth and started to push me back down—but even with my head spinning, I could tell they were drunk and unsteady. So I bit the hand—which tasted like cigarettes—and they let me go.

I could hear the person lying on the ground moaning, and she sounded like a woman. The guy tried to shove me and grab my parka at the same time, but as I was on the other side of the person on the ground, I broke away and staggered down the alley running my hands along the wall while I heard him swearing behind me. In two seconds, the fog cleared, and I could see the bakery.

I didn't look back. I walked as quickly as I could to the screen door, swung the other door closed, locked it, and walked straight into Dad. "Why are you locking the door..." and as he looked down at me, he saw the red mark on my forehead, the look on my face, and a bit of blood on my coat. He grabbed me and shook me and said, "What happened?"

I started to feel sick, and I could taste a little bit of blood in my mouth, and I started to cry—he shook me again and said, "Cathy! What happened?" I told him about the movie and the alley, and the guy, and before I could finish, he grabbed me by the arm and walked me up the stairs.

He yelled "Lola!" and it must have been the way he said it because Mom jumped up out of her chair and walked into the kitchen, took one look at him and one look at me, and said, "What happened?"

And as Dad and I were trying to tell her, she tilted my face up to look at my forehead, and unzipped my parka to have a look at my clothes. Mom pulled up my sweater, and checked that my pants were buttoned and the zipper in my pants was up. She told me to go and get into the shower, and wash my face and the inside of my mouth, and then brush my teeth. I started to ask why, and she yelled "GO!" and as I was taking off my clothes in the bathroom I could hear her screaming at Dad, and him yelling back.

I started to cry for real now, as I started the shower and made it as hot as I could. I scrubbed my face and even wiped the bar of Zest with my finger, and washed out my mouth. When I got out of the shower, they were still yelling, and David and Richard had come upstairs to join in. Dad was telling them to go out to the alley to see if someone was still there, and they said that he should call the RCMP, and they didn't want anything to do with those crazy drunks, and what if one of them had a knife? I sat on the toilet and listened for a while, until I heard them move into the living room. I wrapped a towel around me, grabbed my clothes—including my parka—and put them on top of the washing machine, and went into my room to change. I didn't understand why everyone was freaking out. I only had a little bump on my head.

Mom came in after a little while with two Anacin and asked me if my head hurt. She had a look and said I might have a black eye tomorrow. She said that she was sorry, and that I wasn't supposed to go through that alley again.

I started to say that I had been through that alley a million times, but she gave me a look, and I stopped talking.

She asked me if I wanted Chinese food for dinner, as she would send David to get it, and I said sure, because I *loved* Chinese food from the café. Dad was lying on the couch sleeping when I went into the living room to see if football was on, and a few minutes later I heard David clomping up the stairs. As soon as the door opened I could smell the delicious, greasy smell of Chinese food. The café specialty was egg rolls that were as big as a medium-sized aluminum container. They were sliced, and when you poured plum sauce from those little packages all over them, they were delicious!

The bag full of food was *huge*. David looked at me out of the corner of his eye, as he was unpacking the food and putting each container onto the countertop, and when he was finished, he really looked at me, with a sort of pained look on his face. Before I could move, David had grabbed my chin and tilted my face up. He brushed my bangs off my forehead to look at the red bump that was forming and said that I was going to have a black eye for sure tomorrow.

Still looking at me, pulling my face a little closer to his, he said, "Cathy... you had better stay out of that alley."

Cutting off My Boot

AFTER THE CHRISTMAS break, Brownies started again. I *loved* going to Brownies. The uniforms, the badges, the ceremonies—and especially the leaders, who were there to talk to you and teach you about service to the community, and the importance of charity, and of being good to the others in your pack.

I met a girl at Brownies who didn't go to the same school as I did. I think she went to private school or was homeschooled. Her name was Alannah. She was taller than I was, perhaps a year older. She had long legs and arms, a beautiful open smile, and huge glasses with thick lenses. Alannah was always laughing. I believe she was the only child of a single mother. Her mother had a cool job—she worked for CBC Radio North, and she did a radio show in the evening. I think it was on jazz music or classical music?

Mr. Xavier always had the radio tuned to CBC in the bakery so they could listen to the news, and I remember I never knew any of the songs they played, and there was always such a long story about the song or the songwriter before they even played the song (and I usually lost interest.). But now that I had a radio in my room, I told Alannah one night at Brownies that I was going to definitely listen to her mom on the radio. That night at Brownies Alannah wasn't feeling well, and one of our leaders put their hand on her forehead and said that she thought that she may have a fever and that she should sit out the rest of the games and rest. They would call her mom to pick her up early. A little while later, her mom walked in, and she had a chat with one of the leaders. While they were talking, Alannah ran over to me and grabbed my arm and said that she wanted me to meet her mom.

Alannah's mom was beautiful. She had shoulder-length dark hair and dark eyes. She had makeup on and a long dark coat over a flowered dress and knee-high boots with heels. She reminded me of David's old girlfriend, Sandy. I still remember how beautiful her voice was when she said hi to me. It was low and soft, and you could almost see it flowing out of her mouth in a chocolaty ribbon as she told me that Alannah had told her that we were quite new to Yellowknife and that my dad was a baker. And then she invited me over for a visit. I said that I would ask my mom, but I was sure it would be OK. I had visions of dinner at Barbara Hilland's house, with the vegetables cut into thin strips… And then she spun around and gathered up her daughter, and Alannah waved as they left the community center.

Before we went home for the night, we all played a game where all the girls sat on the floor in two rows with their legs stretched out in front of them, with the same number of girls on the other side facing each other. When the music started the two girls at the end would run around the backs of the sitting girls, and try to run in between all the girls' legs and sit back down, while the next two girls did the same thing until all the girls had a turn.

Some of the girls had indoor shoes that they changed into when they arrived for Brownies each week, but I didn't, instead wearing my big, brown, fake suede boots with fake sherpa trim, with brown laces up the front and sort of a platform crepe-sole. I also didn't have any socks on, as the inside of the boots were made of the fake sherpa, and I loved how cozy they felt. As we were all wearing knee-length brown skirts as part of our Brownie uniform, some of the girls also had on brown or skin-colored tights to keep their legs warm. Not me. I hated the way tights felt. They were too hot and scratchy, so I was bare legged in my boots.

When it was my turn to run, I was worried about stepping on some poor girls leg with my big boots, so I had to hop over a couple of pairs of legs at a time, and at some point fell over and twisted my ankle. When I tried to get up, I couldn't, and it really hurt, and one of our leaders said that that she would call the bakery and have someone pick me up and take me to the hospital emergency room.

David arrived, helped me into the bakery van, and drove me to the emergency room. There was nobody in there, so the nurse told David to lift me up onto one of the beds in the back, and the doctor came over and asked me what happened. I started to tell him the whole long story about the game, and the girls legs, and the whole time he was looking at my right leg and my boot. When I stopped talking he asked me if my boots had zippers at the back, and I said that they were slip-ons, and he said he needed to take off my boot to see my ankle, and he and the nurse tried to pull my boot off.

I needed to bend my ankle to pull off my boot, and my feet were all sweaty, and my ankle was already starting to swell—after another try, and a cry of pain from me, he said that he would have to cut my boot off!

Not my boots! I loved those boots! They were the nicest item of clothing I had! I tried to protest and started to cry, but he already had the scissors out, and he cut right down the center, from knee to toes, and as they removed my beloved boot I could see my red and purple, bruised and swollen ankle.

After a bit more poking and prodding, as well as an x-ray, he told me that no bones were broken. I asked if I was getting a cast? (the only thing that could improve this night) He said no; he would wrap my ankle and give me a set of crutches, and I should not put any weight on it for the next day or two. My stinky, sweaty foot was cleaned and wrapped, and the crutches were handed over to David—who tried them out, as he remembered having to use them when he banged up his knee in his car accident in Calgary, and said that they were easy to use. But he said he didn't know how I was going to get up the stairs to the apartment, and I might have to sleep in the bakery van or in the cellar with the rats.

When I started to cry, the doctor took the crutches from him and showed me how to use them and told me to be careful on the ice. David went and got the van and helped me in.

When we got back to the bakery, Dad was standing at the back door. I managed to get out, and between the two of them they got me up the stairs. Mom was sleeping, so I limped my way to my room, got undressed, and propped my ankle up on two pillows that David brought over from their room. With a sigh, I tried to go to sleep.

Puss-Puss was sleeping in her favorite spot above my head in her little canopy/hammock, and as I was trying to get comfortable I heard her stirring. She got up and stretched, like a white Halloween cat, gave a big yawn and a squeak, and carefully made her way along the thin side rail, like a furry tightrope walker, one delicate paw after the other, until she reached the headboard. She looked down at me and gave a little surprised squeak and made her way down towards my propped-up ankle. She carefully sniffed me from the waist down, and when she got to the bandage, she sniffed from one side to the other and looked back at me, probably trying to figure out where I had been and why I smelled funny.

After my bandaged ankle was thoroughly examined by Dr. Pussycat, she turned around three times, flopped down right where the second pillow held up my injured ankle, curled herself into a ball with her back pressed against the lower part of my leg, and proceeded to purr up a storm—doing her part to heal my sprain.

All night long, the door to my room would swing open with a creak, and in would walk Dad, David, Richard, walking to the end of my bed to look at my injured ankle. Each one of them poked my foot in a different spot. David wiggled my big toe, Richard poked the bandage under my pinky toe, and Dad poked the top of my ankle above the bandage. Each time I said "ow," or "ouch," or "that hurts," and each time they would shrug their shoulders and leave, closing the door nearly all the way behind them leaving Puss-Puss and I illuminated by the kitchen stove light (I suppose, for the next time).

I was off school for a few days, and every day Mom would unwrap and re-wrap my ankle depending how swollen it was. She would put ice on it, and in a few days I could get around the apartment without crutches. I kept looking at my single boot sitting in the corner of my room, sad and alone.

As it was spring, I could wear my gum boots to school, and after the streets were a little less lake-like, I could switch to runners—especially as the snow was nearly gone. I went back to Brownies the following week wearing an old pair of flip-flops I had brought from Calgary.

David dropped me off at the community center, and everyone was talking about Alannah. There were a few less girls there than usual, and the leader had us sit on the floor—with me in a chair because of my ankle—and told us that Alannah had been in the hospital since last week and was very, very sick. She had something called "spinal meningitis" and had a very high fever, and a couple of the other girls were also sick with it, but they were much less sick. Our leader told us that Alannah was in isolation in the hospital because this disease was quite contagious, but she was glad to see that the majority of us were fine.

She asked if we had any questions, and of course, we did. One girl wanted to know what contagious meant, and if we could go and visit Alannah in the hospital? We were told that contagious meant that the disease could spread very easily, and that's why she was in isolation, so no one was allowed to visit her—only her mom, and she had to wear a mask and gloves and a hospital gown every time she was in her daughter's hospital room.

I was thinking how Alannah had grabbed my arm last week when she wanted me to meet her mom, and was worried. I started to feel a little hot, and my mouth suddenly went dry. I must have gone quite pale, so our leader gave my leg a pat and said that as we had all gone a week without symptoms that we were all going to be fine, and that one of our projects for tonight was going to be making Alannah a get-well-soon card from all of us—from her pack.

SNOWMOBILING IN THE BUSH

THE LAST OF the snow continued to hang on, and we had flurries nearly every day as April turned to May. One day after school, Doug asked if I would like to go snowmobiling with him and his brothers on Saturday.

The only thing I knew about snowmobiles had to do with that poor kid in our class whose dad had been killed by a polar bear, and I suppose I looked a little worried. Doug must have noticed and said that it was daylight most of the day now, and we would be with his brothers, and that I could wear his mom's ski-doo suit, and it would be fun... so I said sure.

I showed up at his house after lunch on Saturday, and I saw his dad's truck parked out front, complete with a trailer containing two yellow and black snowmobiles. Everything about them reminded me of big fat bumblebees, including the rounded script reading "Ski-Doo" on the side. The front door was open, and I saw Doug exiting the front door with a huge pile of something that looked like puffy comforters (except for the color, which was a neon orange), which turned out to be four ski-doo suits that we would wear when we were riding.

I waved, and I saw his hand go up over top of the pile, and in frustration (or just because he was a boy), he flung the entire pile into the front yard, and one by one they slid down the icy slope to the road, right behind the trailer.

His brothers came running out of the house, followed by the huge dogs, and one of them ran up into the backyard to fence them in, and the other brother ran down to the truck, and screamed at Doug to pick up the ski-doo suits before they got wet, get them into the back of the truck, and get in, as we should get going. I was standing at the door of the truck ready to do my part to get us going, and the brother next to the truck lifted me up into the back seat and piled two ski-doo suits on top of me. Doug scrambled in the other side with the other two suits. The truck was started and we were off.

We drove for about a half an hour, down through old town with all the little multicolor houses and out past Prelude Lake. The snow kept falling, and the sky was a sort of white/blue, but not stormy. We pulled onto a side road, and drove for a while longer. Doug and I were bouncing around in the back on the rough road, and I couldn't stop thinking about the kid from school and his dad. I was glad it wasn't dark, and I was hoping that the polar bears were still sleeping in their dens.

The truck came to a stop, and we all got out, and Doug's brothers started the procedure to unhook the snowmobiles from the trailer and ease them down onto the snowy road. Doug was busily sorting through the ski-doo suits, trying to find the name written on the inside neck of each suit. He found his mom's suit and tossed it my way. I must have looked confused as what to do next, so he told me to sit in the truck and take my boots off, and get my legs in the suit, and then I would put on his mom's boots, and stand up, and see if I could zip up the suit with my parka on—otherwise to take off my parka and just wear the suit. My parka did fit inside, so he helped me pull out my hood and made sure I was zippered up, and told me to wait until the boys had their suits on so they could tell me the rules.

The suit was so padded, I felt like the Michelin Man—I could barely move my arms. I felt like a little baby that was wearing a onesie snowsuit, and ended up looking like a gingerbread man cookie spread out on a pan. Doug's mom's boots were also a little snug, and as they laced up to the knee, I couldn't imagine how far I would get if I had to walk anywhere. Doug said that because we would be going kind of fast on the snowmobiles, that we had to be careful our toes and fingers didn't get frostbitten. And with that, he handed me a pair of mittens to match the neon orange suit.

When Doug's brothers were dressed, they came around the side of the truck to see if we were ready, and when they saw the two of us, they started to laugh. They were used to seeing Doug, but I guess the two of us together must have looked comical. Once they stopped laughing, they inspected our suits and boots and mitts, and even though it was probably only minus 15 or 20, with very little wind, they looked at me and told me the rules.

Rule number one was that we were to stay behind them on the trail. Doug would be driving the snowmobile I was on, as he needed to practice, but under no circumstances were we to veer off the trail. If it started to snow really hard, and the track was hard to see, we were to speed up a bit, and they would slow down. If something happened with the snowmobile and it stopped, we were supposed to stay put, and they would follow the trail back to us.

Lastly, they asked me if I had to pee and were sorry that they forgot to ask me earlier, but it was OK if I had to, and they pointed towards a little bush, and said I could go over there. And then the three of them burst out laughing! I said I didn't have to pee, and they said we should get going and to remember the rules.

Doug didn't need to be told twice. He hopped on the snowmobile and turned the key, and it started right up. I waddled over to the back, and tried to swing my leg over the back seat and slide on. After the second try, Doug yelled over the sound of the engine that I should bend my knee onto the seat, and once I was half on, swing my leg around, and that worked, somehow. He told me to hold onto him and asked if I was ready. I nodded my head, then realized he couldn't see me, as I was behind him, so I yelled "Yes!"

One of his brothers raised his arm in the air and took off, while Doug did the same as the brother on the back of the other snowmobile gave a yell, and we were off.

I had never been on a motorcycle, but I imagined that it would be a similar feeling. I tried to hang on to Doug as we went down and up little hills and around corners—temporarily losing sight of his brothers, but as Doug sped up, I caught a glimpse of neon orange and knew they were close. It was strangely quiet, except for the engine. The white of the snow combined with the neon of the suits was hard on my eyes, which were already watering from the breeze created as we zipped along.

I was nice and warm, and after a while when Doug would stand up as we were going down a hill, I started standing too. Although we couldn't speak, I could tell that he was loving driving the snowmobile, even though to me it looked so uncomfortable, as he had to stretch his arms so far out to the sides to steer through the surprisingly deep snow and occasionally squeeze the brakes.

After a while, I had no idea how long we'd been out there, zipping past scrubby trees, and once spotting a big white hare. I must have started to get sleepy. I loosened my grip on Doug and found myself sliding right off the back seat, landing flat on my back onto the snow. I remember listening to the sound of the ski-doo as it got farther and farther away and feeling so comfortable lying there in the white stillness with snowflakes falling slowly onto my cheeks. I wasn't scared at all, just tired, and it was nice to be still after however long I had sat vibrating from the treads grabbing the snow underneath my seat. It occurred to me that going to sleep might not be a smart thing to do, so I tried to sit up, which was nearly impossible from the lying position I was in. I tried rolling to one side to try to push myself up, but the snow was soft, so I couldn't manage that either. I ended up rolling all the way over on my stomach, with my face turned to the side, and somehow managed to push myself up into a kneeling position—but as I had nothing to grab onto, had no idea how I was going to get to my feet, especially in Doug's mom's ginormous boots.

As I was rolling around in the snow like a beached whale, imagining the ravens laughing at me if they happened to be flying by, I thought that getting up after you fall off the snowmobile should have been part of the rules. I was considering unzipping my suit and ditching my gloves in order to gain a little more flexibility when I heard the sound of an engine and three voices yelling, "Cathy!" and I knew I was saved.

I knew I looked stupid, crouched as I was on all fours, so I decided to flip myself over on my back until someone arrived to pull me up. I started to yell "Over here!" but I remembered that they would be following the track back to find me. I kept yelling anyway: "Oveeerrrrr heeeerrreee!"

In a few minutes they arrived, and the next thing I knew, all three boys were pulling me up and brushing me off. Doug was white as a sheet, and I felt bad that he had been so scared that he had lost me. They kept asking me if I was OK, and I said it was all my fault because I had accidentally loosened my grip.

I asked how long it had been before Doug realized I was gone, and both boys gave him a look and said that it had been at least half an hour, and I was very lucky that I was OK. I told them I was fine, still warm and everything. I was sorry that they had been worried. They said it was OK, and that we should be heading back anyway.

One of Doug's brothers tugged on my sleeve and motioned me over to his snowmobile, and lifted me onto the front, and for a minute I thought, *I don't know how to drive this thing*, but as he was so tall, he just reached his arms out and grabbed the handlebars, and we were off. As we drove past the second snowmobile, I saw a very long-faced Doug climbing onto the back as his brother steered onto the trail behind us.

I Didn't Want To
Be a Woman

I HAD FINISHED reading almost everything in the young adult section at both the library and the school library, and I started to stray into the teen section of the library down the street. I read a terrifying book called *Go Ask Alice*, about a runaway who develops a drug problem. The descriptions of the crazy trips she had on acid, LSD, or whatever gave me nightmares for weeks. Next, I read *The Bell Jar* by Sylvia Plath, and that started out all right, but when she started to lose her mind and contemplate suicide, I felt obligated to go along with her and finish the book—again, my kindness got me nothing but nightmares.

I don't know if it was the books or the stress of having two grown men show up in the bodies of my brothers, but I also experienced a daytime nightmare, one that would go on each month for the next 45 years—I got my period a month or two after I turned 11.

I had been reading Judy Blume, and one of the books (I can't remember which one) described how much the character in the book—Margaret?—wanted to get her period, as all her 15-year-old friends were getting it. To her, it was one of the signs that she was turning from a girl into a young woman. I couldn't relate to any of that. I was a kid and happy to be one.

It started sort of gradually, with dark brown/rusty red stains on my underwear. I thought I must be dying, so I took off the offending garment, and walked over to Mom's chair to show her when Dad and the boys were at work. She knew what was happening and walked me into her room and fished out of her packed suitcase a sort of elastic belt thing and a thick white pad with pieces of fabric at each end. She handed them to me, and told me that she could show me how to put it on (No, thank You!) and said that I couldn't just wear a pad in my underwear, as it could fall out onto the floor for everyone to see—and as it would be filled with blood, it would be very unhygienic. I just could not believe what she was saying!

She said that once a month I would bleed for a few days, and maybe get a few cramps in my stomach, and looked at me when she told me that *I would have to be careful now, because I could get pregnant*—and then turned and walked away. I stood there stunned halfway between the bathroom and the washing machine and thought, *no way*. No way was I doing a period. I certainly had no idea how I could get pregnant and didn't want to know. So I put my dirty underwear back on, closed the Judy Blume book, and put it back into my book return bag—Judy Blume was now dead to me—and threw the pad and elastic belt thing in my little trash can, and went out to see Doug.

A few days later, at school, I went to the bathroom and saw that my underwear and the inside of my jeans were soaked with blood. Bright red blood that smelled like the oil barrel sort of metal. For a minute, sitting there on the toilet, trying to figure out if I should scream or cry, the room started to spin, and I thought I saw spots before my eyes just like Mom at the plant nursery in Calgary. I sat there with my eyes closed until the sick feeling passed.

My stomach was aching, the inside of my stomach, deep in my body. I had never experienced that kind of pain before, and I had absolutely no idea what I was going to do. I sat there for—I don't remember how long, listening to the blood plop drop by drop into the water in the toilet. I kept using the toilet paper but I just kept bleeding and feeling sick and dizzy. By this time, my stomach was throbbing so bad I could feel the pain in my back teeth—or maybe that was because I was clenching my jaw so tightly. I started to rock back and forth, and thought that if I could stuff my underwear with toilet paper and manage to stand up, I could pull up my pants and head straight out the front door, walk home, and try to find that stupid pad-thing my mom had given me, and lie down.

When I finally got up, I was doubled over. I slowly straightened up and flushed the toilet about five times to hide the evidence, then walked over to the sink to wash my hands that were covered with blood. I took off my cardigan and tied it around my waist, to hide the top of my pants, and walked out into the hall just as the bell rang. I turned towards the door, and as the kids streamed out of their classrooms, I fainted.

When I woke up, there were two teachers standing over me and they helped me sit up, and one of them gave me some water. They asked me if I thought I could stand up, and I said yes, and I sat on a chair in the office while they called the bakery to have someone pick me up. A few minutes later I saw the blue bakery van pull up to the front door, and a minute later Dad walked in looking a bit worried. When I saw him, I almost started to cry. He had a few words with the teacher, looked over at me, and said "C'mon." I was worried that I had left a puddle of blood on the floor and the chair, so I practically ran out to the van.

I don't know what the teacher said to him, but he opened my door and dug around on the floor for an old towel that they used to clean the van windows when it got mucky out—he laid it on the seat and told me to get in, and I thought I would die of embarrassment.

We didn't say a word on the ride back. When I got out, I took the dirty towel with me—I knew I had lots of things to wash, and wondered if bloodstains came out of clothing. I ran up the stairs and into my room to change. Mom came into my room with a couple more pads, and asked again if I needed her to show me how to put the elastic belt thing on. I grabbed the pads and screamed "No!" and slammed the door after she left.

When David and Richard got finished work and saw me standing at the washing machine, each of them took turns hissing something nasty in my direction—like I better watch myself because now that I was "on the rag" boys would be able to smell me and want to do all sorts of things to me, and I better watch it or I would get "knocked up"—until Mom yelled at them from her chair to leave me alone.

I kept thinking how Doug was a boy and my friend, and I started to worry that everything was going to change.

BICYCLES—AGAIN

THE SNOW WAS finally gone, and the ground dried up, and the sun was shining so kids were starting to ride their bikes. I had no idea what had happened to my Calgary bike, and I must have asked Mom and Dad a million times and never got an answer. Everyone was riding their bikes to school, and I was still on foot, grumbling all the way. Summer break was coming, and I knew that if Doug, Scott, and Gillian were riding to the lake to swim or to the tennis courts or just around town, I wouldn't be able to join them without a bike. I did NOT want to go back to being friendless.

My whining must have worked. Dad was doing well as bakery manager, so one day I came home from school and walked through the bakery to say hi to Mr. Xavier before he went home for the day, and everybody was acting weird. They were all looking at me and smiling, except Dad, of course. He reserved his smiles for someone who could do something for him, like Mary in the coffee shop who always saved him a piece of his favorite pie. Dad walked over to me and told me to come with him to the garage. Everyone was still looking at me, so I followed him, and in the corner was a cardboard box—he pointed to the box and told me that he had bought me a bike!

I examined the box, but couldn't understand how a bike could be in a small rectangular box. He said that this was a special bike, it was a new thing, a folding bike, and that Richard would put it together for me. I just stared at him, and looked back at everybody standing in the doorway smiling.

David said "I told you she wouldn't like it!"

I took a closer look at the box and crouched down to examine the picture. It looked a little strange, and it was white, not red, with no sissy bar or red metallic banana-seat. But hey, I was getting older, and maybe the other kids would think this bike was cool—so I stood up and asked Dad when he could put it together, and thanked him, and I managed a weak smile.

David snorted, and walked back into the bakery, and Dad said Richard would put it together after work—but he looked a little disappointed that I wasn't more excited, and that made me feel bad. I didn't understand why he just didn't go to Marshall Wells or the Bay and get me a regular bike.

A few days later (after some persistent nagging on my part), the bike was put together. It was more complicated than a regular bike, so I remember David giving up on assembling this weird bike and I saw Richard crouched down in the garage on and off for a couple of days putting it together. But eventually, it was finally ready to ride.

It was white, and had a regular black seat, and was pretty small, but it fit me well. It had two sets of hinges so the bike could be folded in three—even with the wheels, I guess you could store it in a small locker, or put it in a car trunk, or in an apartment. I took it out for a spin in the back alley, and by the time I had driven to the end of the alley, onto the street, behind Marshall Wells, past the Bay, and down the other end of the alley, I decided that despite its looks, this was going to be a good bike for me.

Dad stood in the alley watching me bike "the loop" and looking pleased. He said something like "It's good, eh?" and I nodded as I stopped briefly in front of him and took off for one more loop.

The bike lived in the garage in front of the blue bakery van, and it wasn't even a week later that my brand-new bike was stolen. I was distraught. I blamed myself for not parking it in the bakery, although I had tried that a couple of times. Every time it was in somebody's way, and they would knock it over and scream upstairs for me to move my damn bike. It was too heavy (even folded up) to drag up the stairs, so the morning it went missing I knew it was gone for good. People used to regularly come into the bakery through the back screen door and steal anything they could carry out... my bike must have been a real prize. I sat on the steps leading into the garage and cried, and Dad told me that he would send a couple of the guys out to look for it, and I should go to school.

Walking seemed like a real chore, after one week with a bike, and I sulked, and moped, and was unhappy for many weeks afterwards. I knew that we couldn't afford another bike. Everything in Yellowknife was at least double the price it had been in Calgary, especially in the winter, before the ice was thick enough to safely drive the ice road across Great Slave Lake—so a new bike was not in the cards, and I knew it.

Word got out at school that my fancy new bike had been stolen. Some kids told me that someone had probably taken it to Edmonton to sell it because I was sure to spot someone else riding it in town. Someone else said that their dad was an RCMP officer and asked if I had a picture of it (which I didn't) because they could put up a STOLEN poster of it at the detachment, just in case my bike ended up in Fort Rae or Hay River. Mostly, kids said that they would keep an eye out for it... but the way they said it, I knew that I would never, ever see that bike again. I started to hate Yellowknife and its stupid bike thieves.

When summer break started, I started spending all my time outside. I would regularly wake up at 2:30 a.m. and think that I should walk down to the tennis courts with my old wooden tennis racket and one tennis ball, and practice hitting the ball over the net, or against the wooden backboard. Sometimes Mom or Dad were awake, drinking coffee in the living room—Dad getting ready to start work, or Mom sleepless as usual. In Yellowknife, 2:30 a.m. was bright, sunny daylight, so it didn't seem strange at all.

Doug and I met up a couple of times at the tennis court, and so did Gillian and I. Apparently she had taken lessons in South Africa, so she always beat us. If I got tired later in the day, I could always have a nap. Yellowknife in July was the definition of the endless summer.

One morning, I was heading out to the library after breakfast, and Dad was standing just outside the screen door smoking. When he saw me, he said "C'mere," and I walked with him to the back corner of the store room—and there was a bike. It wasn't my stolen bike. This bike was a ten-speed girls' bike that was painted a sort of metallic fuchsia purple, with a seat to match. It had chrome bumpers and skinny tires, and it was beautiful!

I stared at the bike, and then I stared at him and said, "Whose bike is that?" He looked away and said that some kid had left it in the alley and asked him to buy it off him, and Dad asked him how much he wanted for it, and he said he would have to ask his sister, but he would come back in a couple of days to let him know... and I knew he was lying. Then he told me that if the kid didn't come back, I could keep the bike.

I had no idea what the real story was, but there was no way I was going to look a gift bike in the mouth. The bike stayed in the back corner for a week, until Dad said that the kid never come back, and David pumped up the tires, and I drove it out the back door and swore that this bike was never going to leave my sight.

I drove the bike over to Gillian's as soon as I got the OK from Dad, and everyone was there. Gillian, Doug, Scott, and Billy. Billy was the son of the minister at the United church, but you would never know it—he was just a regular kid. The three boys had set up a wooden bike ramp looking thing out of scrap wood, old pallets, and an old piece of plywood. It was a nice hot day, and Gillian and I were sunning ourselves on her front lawn while the boys were busy building and tweaking the ramp across the street in the shade. They would take turns riding their bikes up the ramp and landing hard on the other side, and sometimes wiping out. The ramp wasn't super high, and they tried to reset it up before every jump. They would yell at us to watch when one of them was sure they were going to make an epic jump.

This went on for an hour or so, and then Billy's last jump practically destroyed the ramp, and he did an epic jump, with an equally epic wipeout afterwards. As he laid flat on his back, his bike beside him with the tire still spinning, Doug and Scott had joined us in the sun, and yelled to check that Billy was OK. He moaned theatrically and said he was just going to lay there for a while, dying... I think Scott and Doug had to go, so they both rode past Billy who was still on the ground, and asked him if he needed a doctor, and they all laughed. Billy moaned and laughed, and Gillian and I continued to chat and tan.

From time to time we yelled over for Billy to get up and come over and join us, but he stopped answering us, so we thought he had fallen asleep. He had gotten so quiet that eventually Gillian said we should check on him.

When we went over to where he was laying, we yelled at him to wake up sort of to scare him, but he didn't move. I leaned down to shake him, both of us saying, "Hey Billy, wake up!" When Gillian shook his shoulder, I could see his t-shirt had sort of ridden up, and there was a huge red and purple bruise that covered almost his whole stomach. We both stood up and looked at each other. My mom had been a nurse, so I asked an obvious question: "Is he still breathing?"

Gillian crouched down and put her ear near his nose and said, "Yes, a little bit."

Gillian's house was empty; her folks had taken her sister for a drive. The street was completely empty, and I said that she should go inside and call an ambulance, and I would run out to the main road to see if I could flag someone down. We both ran in opposite directions, and when I got to the road I could see only one car coming towards me—a small, green, compact car, with a woman driving. I walked out into the middle of the road and waved my hands, and as she got closer, she honked her horn and was waving me off the road. I screamed that I needed help, that someone was hurt, and she slowed the car and rolled down the window and asked what was wrong.

I told her about Billy and the bike ramp, and motioned towards poor Billy lying on the grass behind me, and she said that she was a nurse on her way to work and told me to get out of the way. She wheeled her car down the street, with me running after it, and stopped the car (but kept it running). Gillian ran out of her house to say that she had called an ambulance but couldn't remember her address, so had a glance at her house number and ran back inside to tell the ambulance dispatcher where she lived.

The nurse crouched down and slapped Billy's face a couple of times and said "Billy, Billy, wake up Billy." and when she lifted up his t-shirt and saw the bruise, and the bike, and the ramp, she told me to get my friend because we were all going to put him in her back seat, and we couldn't wait for the ambulance.

Gillian came out of the house screaming that the ambulance lady thought she was pulling a prank and hung up on her. I screamed for her to come over and help us, as this lady was a nurse. We had to get Billy in the car, and she would drive him to the hospital. The nurse opened the back seat, and threw everything on the floor, and told us that we needed to pick him up carefully and not drop him, and that he might yell but to just head for the car. We should put as much of his body on the backseat as we could, then she would run around to the other side and help us pull him all the way in.

I was the smallest, so I took his legs, and Gillian and the nurse put their hands underneath his middle, the nurse supporting his chest and head, and Gillian his stomach and hips. On three, we lifted, and Billy let out a yell, and I almost let go, and the nurse screamed "Move!" and we all walked towards the car. I put his legs on the seat, ran around the other side, and started to pull them towards the driver's seat door. Somehow Gillian and the nurse managed to get a yelling, squirming Billy into the back seat. The nurse ran around to my side and bent Billy's legs, rested them against the seat, and slammed the door.

As Gillian looked older than me, the nurse asked her to get into the front seat as she would need Billy's last name and some other information when they got to the hospital. She asked me if I knew where he lived, and I said I thought he lived near the church, and I pointed towards the steeple. She told me to bike over there and find Billy's parents and tell them to get to the hospital, and to tell them that she thought that Billy might have ruptured his spleen. I nodded and gave Gillian a guilty look, wondering how we had been so stupid as to let Billy practically die as we chatted and tanned. But I had no time to think about that now, so I grabbed my bike as the car sped off towards the hospital and pedaled as fast as I could towards the church, praying that Reverend Ormiston—Billy's dad—was there.

Puss-Puss the Hunter

TOWARDS THE END of our time in Yellowknife, Puss-Puss developed a secret life. To the naked eye, she looked to be a regal, tail and head high, part-Persian tortoiseshell princess. She stayed mostly in my bedroom sleeping at the top of the canopy bed, or venturing outside (when the bedroom window wasn't frozen shut) for some fresh air, but when the boys and Dad were working downstairs in the middle of the night, she would sometimes sneak down the long staircase into the bakery.

At the foot of those stairs was another set of three wooden stairs, to a basement-type storage room filled with sacks of flour, carved out of the tundra. There was very little headroom: a problem for the bakers, but not for an eight pound, deceptively vicious fluffy hunter.

The room was nearly the entire footprint of the bakery, dimly lit with a single bare bulb. Puss-Puss had taken to sitting on the bottom basement step each night, waiting to hear some movement. According to Dad—who had watched her slink soundlessly down the stairs followed by a startled *squeak*—she was becoming a master rat catcher. This was evidenced by the orderly display of the night's catch carefully lined up on the top basement stair, waiting for him to come by to inspect.

She never ate the foul creatures, and I don't recall her ever nursing a bite. Dad was by no means a pet person, but smart business practices dictated that less rats meant less flour to buy, so clearly, she had become an asset to the business.

It was several months before I realized that the cat had been doing a night shift in the basement each evening. I had come downstairs late one night, following the smell of sugar and grease to a tray filled with freshly-made glazed donuts, and was shocked to see her there... and even more surprised to see my father carrying a small saucer of cream to the top basement step, complete with a head pat as he tossed the night's catch into the back alley for the ravens. Puss-Puss would finish the cream like the most pampered of felines, not a flour-covered ratter sitting on a bare wooden basement step. After a stretch, she would wander back up the stairs, like one of the bakers clocking out after the nightshift, and silently pad back to my/her room as dawn was breaking. A graceful leap onto the canopy, a couple of turns to get settled, and she would spend the next 30 minutes using her rough tongue to clean the cream off of her whiskers and paws, along with any cobwebs, and occasionally a drop or two of rodent blood that may have soiled her fur during what I can only imagine to have been many epic battles between feline and prey.

I Want To Go Home

THREE THINGS HAPPENED when summer turned to fall: I moved schools and started grade six, I got caught hitchhiking, and we had a family meeting (the first of many) to decide whether or not we should buy the Gold Range Hotel.

The new school was very close to my old school, but it was an old stone two-story building that looked like every other school in Canada. I continued to hang with Doug, Gillian, Scott, and Billy. I met another great teacher—who I learned a lot from, and who, like my former teacher, guided me through what was continuing to be a difficult transition from Calgary to Yellowknife.

Doug continued to be my friend, and I continued to be obnoxious in my telling and retelling of the fantastic life I had left behind. One day we were walking to his place after school, and as usual, something someone had done or said had reminded me of Calgary, and I was babbling on about it. Doug stopped, and I stopped walking and talking, and he looked at me and said, "If Calgary is so great, why don't you just go back there?"

For a split second I thought I would faint or cry or throw up. He must have seen me go pale. Uttering the sentence out loud was like a slap; it was the absolute meanest, most truthful thing he could have said. In that moment he realized that we both knew that I could never go back, and by pointing it out, he had made me feel unwelcome in Yellowknife. I just stood there, blinking.

He told me he was sorry, but he just didn't understand why I didn't *love* how great Yellowknife was. I told him that I had to go, and I turned around to walk towards the bakery. I could hear him say, "Cathy!" a couple of times, but I kept walking as a couple of tears rolled down my face.

In that moment, I wanted to run away. I wanted David to pull up in the GTO or the Camaro and tell me to "Get in!" and take me to Dairy Queen or to Boogie's for a burger. I wanted him to drive really fast, and I wanted to close my eyes, and when I opened them to be on John Laurie Boulevard and see the brown softness of Nose Hill. I wanted to go home.

On Saturday morning I left the apartment with a small bag containing a couple of donuts and a book. I kissed Puss-Puss goodbye and started walking towards the airport, which would lead me to the edge of the lake and the ferry. I would sneak on with the other passengers and find my way back to Calgary.

I probably walked for two hours or so. I was just getting to the long hill past the construction site where they were finishing the new Explorer Hotel, and I turned around and stuck out my thumb and walked a bit more, wondering why I didn't bring any water with me. About half way down the hill, I turned around to face the oncoming traffic, and stuck out my thumb—but the only vehicle coming my way was a blue van.

For a split second, I thought I should just dive into the brush beside the road, and roll down the big hill and plunge myself into the water below because I saw Dad driving the bakery van straight at me.

As he slowed down and pulled over with a squeal, I could see the red brake lights come on as he stopped. All I could think of was that day so long ago when I had looked out of Barbara Hilland's front window and seen him pacing up and down Norquay Drive calling my name.

I just stood there staring at the van, until finally, like a prisoner on the way to the gallows, I walked as slowly as I could over to the passenger side door, with my head down. I was finally realizing how exhausted I was by the walk with only a couple of glazed donuts to sustain me.

When I got to the door, the window was open, and I looked at Dad, and all he said was, "Get in."

I opened the door and got in, and he turned his head to check for cars coming up behind him and pulled onto the road. He looked so funny sitting there in the van, like the cab was too small for him, with his head nearly touching the ceiling. He stared straight ahead, and I could tell that he was mad, but I could also tell that he was trying not to show it.

"Where were you going?" was his first question.

I burst into tears and told him that I *hated* Yellowknife and that I was walking to the ferry and was going to hitchhike back to Calgary. He nodded his head and asked who would look after Mom, and I cried harder and screamed that *he* should be looking after Mom, and I wanted to go home.

Dad took a breath and kept driving past Prelude Lake, and he told me that he was working on a deal to buy the hotel next door, and that Mom was getting better, and as soon as he had a bit more money, he was going to buy a house for Mom and me. I wanted to know if we could buy our old house, and he said that we would see—but he and Mom had been talking, and he thought that we would probably move to a small town that they had visited when we lived in North Vancouver. It was called Abbotsford, and if everything went well, I could probably start grade seven there.

I told him that I wanted to go back to Calgary, and he said that we would see. He would have a talk with Mom about it. He sounded so reasonable, and I had stopped crying, and he handed me a half full bottle of Coke that was in the cup holder, and I drank it.

Dad turned the van around, pulled over, and put it in park. He kept the engine running, and for the first time, he turned his body to face me. He told me that I had to be patient for a little longer and not try to leave just yet, that he had a plan, and everything was going to work out, but I needed to keep helping Mom. Especially if we bought the hotel because he and the boys would be working all the time, and she would need me.

He looked old. He looked tired. He looked like he needed me to do what he wanted me to do, so I said, "OK." He turned back to the front, put the van into drive, and we headed back to the bakery.

THE GOLD RANGE HOTEL

IN OCTOBER OR November, the family meeting was called. I couldn't remember the last time we had all been in the same room together, but you could tell that no one wanted to be there except for Dad. He started laying out his plan, and I tried to pay attention, but almost nothing applied to me, except that I was going to be given a few shares (whatever they were), and I would have to sign some papers at the lawyers, and if everything went well, we would be hotel owners before Christmas.

I looked around the room and no one looked happy. Everyone looked worried, but Dad kept saying that if we worked hard, we would make a go of it. He said that the books looked good and that this was a great deal. Then he asked us to vote. No discussion, no questions.

I think everyone said, "yah," and I even put up my hand in agreement.

That was it. The meeting was over. And the rest, as they say... is history.

The winter passed with a steady flow of activities. The hotel deal was finalized, and so I had somewhere else to explore. The hotel lobby was something out of an old movie. The front desk had a *huge* machine with red and white wires, and holes, and plugs, which Dad told me was a switchboard. One Saturday afternoon he gave me a five-minute lesson on how it worked, and told me that answering the calls could be my job if I wasn't needed to slice bread in the bakery. (I hated slicing bread—the breadcrumbs would get under my sleeves and make me itchy, and ever since the Aunty Ann and the knife incident, I wasn't too keen to be operating a machine with 25 serrated blades bouncing up and down.)

I sat down in the chair, and instantly felt like I was on the bridge of the Starship Enterprise—there were so many moving parts. Dad said that when someone called, I was to say, "good morning," or "good afternoon," and then, "Gold Range Hotel, Cathy speaking. How may I help you?" And when the person asked me to connect them to such and such room, I was to grab the white wire out of the hole at the bottom, plug it into the hole of the corresponding room number, and wait for the person to pick up the phone in the room. When they picked up, I was supposed to hang up the phone, and when the light turned off at that room I could unplug the wire and put it back in the hole at the bottom.

If someone from one of the rooms upstairs called, I was supposed to take a red wire, and plug it into the flashing room number hole and say the "good afternoon" thing again. Dad said that if the people in the rooms wanted water, ice, or their bed made, or if someone asked for something, I was supposed to take the pink pad of papers that said memos and write down the room number and write down what they wanted, and then call the housekeeper at 100 and tell them. Then he looked at me and said, "OK?" and I nodded.

Dad could do long division in his head. He could manage as many jobs as were hours in the day. I was still trying to figure out which wire went where, and was wondering if I should use a pen or a pencil to write the notes.

I believe I received five or six calls or inquiries that afternoon, and I don't think I got any of them right. I got tired of saying hello and hearing nothing on the other end. I was also unsure when my shift was over, so when Mary walked through the lobby after her shift in the café and told me that there was one piece of lemon pie left in the pie showcase, I immediately abandoned my post (leaving a couple of room lights flashing) and plugged in a few red and white wires into a pattern I thought was pretty. I followed Mary back to the café, where we ate a piece of pie and chatted about my new life as a working girl in a hotel.

DAVID AND PATTY—
AND TRACEY

SPRING WAS AS wet and cold as the year before, but I was excited when David came upstairs one afternoon to tell me that Patty was coming up for a visit and that she was bringing Tracey! In August 1973, Patty—David's wife, whom he was separated from but who was my absolute favorite girlfriend/wife of either brother—had given birth to a baby girl in Edmonton. They had named her Tracey-Lee, and at ten years old, I had become an aunty.

I had never even seen a picture of the baby, and although I was a little jealous that someone younger (and most likely cuter) had joined the family, I was really looking forward to seeing Patty again, and seeing the baby. David said that Patty and him were going to go out one night, and that I should babysit.

Both David and Richard were living in a trailer park outside of town, and I had been to their trailers once or twice. I was excited to babysit, so at the appointed time I hopped into his truck, and we drove out to his trailer.

Patty looked exactly as I remembered her, and she cried a little when she saw me and told me that I would be taller than her soon. She asked me how I liked living in Yellowknife. I managed to tell her a few things I liked, but David interrupted us—he was always in a hurry, always jumpy, always nervous, and often drunk when he wasn't working.

Patty took me into the back bedroom where little tiny Tracey was sleeping on a single bed with a bunch of pillows and blankets all around her. Patty said it was so she wouldn't roll onto the floor by accident. She said that she would probably sleep until they got back in a few hours, but if she started crying, I could take a bottle out of the fridge and put it into the pot of hot water that was on the stove, wait five minutes, and then feed it to her.

I must have looked worried, but Patty gave me a squeeze and said that she was fed and would probably sleep right through, and when David walked down the hall and hissed "C'mon!" she left me standing there.

As he was pulling her down the hall by her hand, she managed to tell me that they were eating at the restaurant at the hotel, so to call if I needed anything. I waved, and after another look at the baby, I headed back to the living room and had a look at the gigantic stereo system and speakers that nearly took up the whole space. After I found the power button and the volume control, I pushed in an 8-track of *Kenny Rogers and the First Edition*, sat down on the couch, and waited for them to come back.

THE FINAL MOVIE

A FEW DAYS later, before Patty flew back to Edmonton, she asked me if I would like to go to the movies with her because Mom was going to look after the baby. She must have seen the look on my face and said, "Don't you like the movies?"

I started to tell her about the curse of the theater, and all the scary movies I had seen there, and she laughed and said that this movie wasn't scary—it was called *The Way We Were* and was a romantic comedy. There would be absolutely no blood or bee stings involved! I was skeptical but said sure, and we headed to the theater.

It was a lovely movie, with lots of kissing and a little bit of fighting and marital problems, but overall the best movie experience by far!

As we walked back to the bakery Patty said that she hoped that she would see me and Mom again soon, but she was pretty sure that she and David were going to get a divorce. I was sad to hear that but said that when I knew where Mom and I were going, I would make sure to phone her, and she said that she had given Mom her phone number. Mom and David and the baby were waiting by the truck when we walked down the alley to the back door of the bakery. Mom gave her and the baby a hug and a kiss, and it was the first time I had seen Mom cry since we had arrived in Yellowknife. We watched them drive off, and Patty took the baby's hand and they waved through the passenger window as David sped off towards the airport, nearly spraying us with stones.

Winnipeg—and Baba—at Last

AFTER SCHOOL WAS out for the summer, Mom said that I was going to Winnipeg for a couple of weeks, and when I got back we would be moving to a new house in Abbotsford, BC. I started asking a million questions, and she told me to get packed for Winnipeg, and she would explain everything when I got back. I was flying in the morning, and Baba was really looking forward to seeing me.

I started packing, and was surprised that I wasn't more excited to be going back to Winnipeg to see everyone. It seemed like a million years since I had been there, and I was more worried than excited. But I was always excited about flying and the airport, so I finished packing and went to bed dreaming about perogies.

The flight was a little longer than it had been from Calgary, and we landed in Edmonton to let on more passengers. I was disappointed we didn't land in Calgary, as I had been half planning my escape. It would take hours before they discovered I got off the plane in Calgary and didn't get back on. I had $50 in my jeans and thought maybe I could get a job at the old bakery, as someone new would have re-opened it by now... or I could hitchhike to Banff and get a job at Phil's or the big hotel.

I was starting to get a little choked up with the realization that none of that was going to work, so by the time the plane left Edmonton, I didn't even want to go to Winnipeg—but I thought that if I died, the only person who would be sad would be Baba, so I tried to cheer up for her sake.

We landed just as a thunderstorm was blowing in, so I hoped whoever was there to pick me up didn't get soaked running from the parking lot to the baggage area. As usual, as I came down the long escalator from arrivals to collect my bags, I scanned the crowd for a familiar face.

I heard a big clap of thunder and saw a blinding bolt of lightning, and the lights flickered, and the escalator shuddered but kept going. The sliding doors into the terminal were stuck closed for a minute as well, and as the rain started to pelt down one of the doors opened, and there was Aunty Mary with her huge purse and her flowing dress, brushing the rain out of her hair and looking around to find me in the crowd.

I yelled "Aunty Mary!" before I could help myself, suddenly so, so, glad to see her, and she looked up with her glasses spotted by the rain and gave a big wave! I waved back, and she walked over to the escalator, and as soon as my feet hit the floor, she gave me a huge hug. She told me how big I had grown and said that she liked my hair long. She put her arm around me and asked me how I was. I almost started to cry from the sheer kindness of it all. A hug, a compliment, someone who was glad to see me? I felt like maybe I should ask if I could just live with her.

My bag came around, and the sky cleared, and the two of us managed to get the bag to the car, and we started to drive the familiar route to Baba's. We chatted the whole way, but as we got closer to Baba's I asked her how long I would have to stay there. She gave me a strange look and said a few days, like always, and that Baba was really looking forward to seeing me. She asked why I asked that question. I didn't know, so I said something about how I was too big to sleep with Baba, and I would rather stay with her or Patty, as there was more to do because I was only there for a few weeks. When the car came to a stop, she said that I could sleep on the couch if I wanted, and she would come back tomorrow, but Baba would be so disappointed if she told her that I wanted to stay with her.

I started to cry, and she asked me what was wrong, and all I could do was shake my head. So she gave me a Kleenex and told me that she would stay for a little while and talk to Baba about what I said.

It was like the happiness of all of the past visits had left me. I was a stranger, and Baba would see that and hate me. I felt like I was too old for Baba, and I hated myself for even thinking that. I walked down the sidewalk to the side door, and when Baba opened the door and saw my face, she grabbed me and hung onto me for at least five minutes while I cried all over her apron. She kept telling me to wait in Ukrainian and led me up the stairs, and when Grampa came towards the kitchen where she had sat me down at the little table, she waved him away with a few hushed words.

Baba sat down in the other chair and looked at me and Aunty Mary, and the two of them had a conversation in Ukrainian while Baba held my hand across the table. Baba said that we should eat, and that after supper I could stay or go—whatever I wanted—and when Grandpa came back to the kitchen, she let him come in, and he took my face in his hands and kissed me and told me that I looked beautiful and that I shouldn't have stayed in "that Yellowknife" for so long.

When he asked about Mom and Dad, Baba said something to him, and he let me go and went into the living room while Baba got Aunty Mary, myself, and her some supper.

Everything was so delicious. Ten times better than I remembered it, as I had been living on veal cutlets and pie... I felt a million times better after I ate, and I asked Baba if I could take a bath and go to bed, and she said sure. And as I walked down to the end of the hall and entered the cleanest, most beautiful bathroom—exactly as I remembered it, with pale pink and black ceramic tile all over the walls—and stepped into the pink bath tub filled with steaming water, I could still hear her and Aunty Mary talking in the kitchen.

The days flew by. I stayed with Baba for a couple of days, and she did what a good Baba does: she gave me a lot of hugs, she let me rest, and she fed me. We talked a little, but nothing was as important as breathing the air in that duplex on McPhillips Street. Air filled with love, the scents of good food, and someone who shared their strength with you. Baba's life had been no bed of roses. I'm sure of that, but she never let me see her struggles. She would have given me her last breath, and even though during the three-hour plane ride and 15-minute car ride to get to her I had forgotten, from the moment she met me at the side door, I knew it. I felt guilty that she was worried about me, but I was worried about me, too.

I felt so strange being there. It came in waves, and I was so incredibly sad that there was even the remote possibility that living in Yellowknife had ruined Winnipeg for me. By the time I had said hi to Sonny and Carol and the cats, and Aunty Mary had walked through the door to take me to her place, I felt as if I was drowning, and I would have to tell one of them in the next 14 days or so that someone needed to save me. When we got in the car, Mary said that if I wanted, she would take me straight over to my cousin Patty's.

Patty was born the same year as Richard, and so that made her 15 years older than me. She was married to a tall, thin architect named Don, and they had a kid and two cats—mother and daughter, Mini and Petite—and a big fluffy dog (who hated me) named King. They lived in a three-story, ramshackle, 100+-year-old house on a tree-lined street with pink peonies in the front flowerbed.

Patty and Don had met at university, and Patty was an artist who worked in clay. Their house was the kind of indescribable chaos that I experienced in many of my family's houses in and around Winnipeg.

Aunty Nancy and Uncle Thor were Patty's parents. Aunty Nancy was the sister closest in age to my mom, and even at 12, I knew that Nancy had been the mother from hell and Patty had spent most of her teenage years trying to get away from her.

All the sisters drank, but Nancy drank like David: deliberately, with purpose, and when the inevitable chaos ensued, she shrugged her shoulders and poured another one. The only difference between them was that Aunty Nancy, along with all the girls, eventually quit drinking…while David did not.

Patty was cheerful like I was—or used to be. She was a giggler; we both were. And although I was serious and always thinking, Patty laughed at everything, and was spontaneous and unapologetic about anything to do with her, her house, and her family.

Walking into that house—compared to the house I grew up in on Norquay Drive—was stimulating. Everywhere you looked, there was color and pattern, and every surface has something to look at. Kids' artwork, paintings on the wall or propped against the wall. Large ceramic pieces, broken or sitting on top of antique furniture she had purchased at weekly auctions with Aunty Mary. Books, dishes, bills, you name it.

When we walked in the front door, Aunty Mary yelled that we had arrived, and Patty's daughter ran into the living room to give her a hug. I noticed a cat perched on one of the stairway posts, who gave a sleepy meow. I almost tripped over the rug in the entrance hall and realized that there were actually three rugs, all different colors, stacked on top of one another, as Patty was still deciding where they should go and which rug she was going to keep.

We walked through the living room into the dining room, a beautiful rectangular room that stretched across the length of the back of the original part of the house—before it was turned into a rooming house for 20-odd years, after which Patty and Don had bought it for cheap with the intention of fixing it up. I was nearly blinded by the sunlight streaming through every pane.

The dining room table was a monster that looked like it belonged in an English manor and was covered in a cotton lace tablecloth that was nearly completely obscured by objects that didn't belong there mixed with some that did. One of the cats was on the table, lapping up the remainder of the milk left in a cereal bowl. *The Winnipeg Free Press* was splayed out at the head of the table, divided into sections, half opened, and the table was surrounded with at least eight chairs—none of which matched. There was a huge sideboard in a different wood and style than the table, piled with bowls, platters, and a large wooden box that probably held an old lady's prized silverware, and in each corner was a china cabinet filled to overflowing with cups and saucers and little do-dads, like silver salt cellars and ceramic representations of oriental cats.

Patty was to the left in her little kitchen washing something out in the sink, and when she saw me, she lifted her wet soapy hands out of the sink and threw them around my neck for a hug and a kiss on the cheek. Aunty Mary said hi to Patty, and when Patty asked if she wanted some tea, Aunty Mary said she couldn't stay. She gave me a big hug, and told me to be good, and she would see me later in the week, while mouthing something to Patty over my head.

I looked at Patty, and she started to laugh, and she said that we should sit down and decide what I wanted to do while I was there. She moved past me into the dining room and started moving the piles of things off the table (and piling them precariously onto the sideboard) and moved a pile of papers off one of the dining room chairs. She gently moved the cat onto the floor, with the cereal bowl, and sat down at the head of the table where the newspaper lay, and asked me how I was.

As the cat finished her milk and started to wind around my legs meowing her Siamese meow, in the background I noticed that the radio was playing in another room, some sort of guitar music, prior to the *bom, bom, bom, "You are listening to CBC radio and I'm Joanne Small with today's headlines."*

I took a deep breath, and as the sunshine in that beautiful, chaotic room covered me like a blanket, I told Patty everything.